WALTHER PPK
SILENCED

The Walther PPK (*Polizeipistole Kriminal* or "Criminal Police Pistol") was a mainstay of German police and military forces during the Second World War – and of agents both real and fictional (it was James Bond's gun) after it. This 1951 silenced version has been modified to allow a leather silencer to be slipped onto the barrel, deadening the sound on firing and with a special chamber to channel the muzzle gases and cool them.

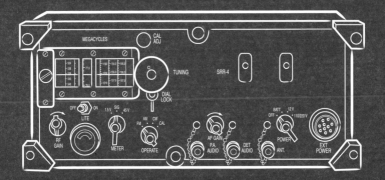

SURVEILLANCE RECEIVER

Developed by the CIA's Office of Technical Services in 1961, the SRR-4 Receiver is able to pick up AM, FM and CW signals enabling monitoring of a wide range of frequencies, including signals from hidden microphones. Lightweight at around 3.5 kg, it was highly portable and could be used for listening from a car or van.

LOCK-PICK KIT

Where agents needed access to secure areas and no accomplice was available, picking locks provided an obvious solution. This lock-pick kit included a variety of picks, wrenches and hooks designed to open most varieties of locks, including pin-tumbler, wafer and lever types. Packed in a small leather case, it weighed less than half a kilogram.

THE COLD WAR SPY POCKET MANUAL

Compiled and Introduced by
Philip Parker

POOLOFLONDON

Philip Parker is a former diplomat and publisher who specialises in the late antique and early medieval periods. He is the author of *The Empire Stops Here: a Journey around the frontiers of the Roman World*, as well as the *Eyewitness Companion Guide to World History*. Philip's most recent book is *The Northmen's Fury: A History of the Viking World*.

This edition published in Great Britain in 2015 by
The Pool of London Press
A Division of Casemate Publishers
10 Hythe Bridge Street, Oxford OX1 2EW, UK
and
1950 Lawrence Road, Havertown, PA 19083 USA

Compilation and introductions © Philip Parker 2015
Volume © Pool of London Press 2015

A CIP record for this book is available from the British Library

ISBN (hardback) 978-1-910860-02-1
ISBN (ebook) 978-1-910860-11-3

Interior designed by BoundUnbound Media.
Endpaper and interior line diagrams by Barking Dog Art
Printed in Finland

Publisher's Note
This compilation contains material of historic interest. The techniques described herein must be considered in the context of their original publication or issue and the publishers exclude liability arising from reliance on the information provided to the fullest extent of the law.

References to material not included from the original in the selected extract have been excluded to avoid confusion. In certain cases superfluous text has been excluded or is missing from the original. This is indicated by a bracketed notation in the text or by the use of an ellipsis. Where text has been redacted from an original document ••••• is used to indicate the censored material.

The Pool of London Press is committed to respecting the intellectual property rights of others. We have therefore taken all reasonable efforts to ensure that the reproduction of all text is done with the full consent of copyright holders. If you are aware of any unintentional omissions, please contact the company so that any necessary corrections can be made for future editions of this book.

To find out more about the Pool of London Press, please visit www.pooloflondon.com and to receive regular email updates on forthcoming Pool of London titles, email info@pooloflondon.com with Pool of London Updates in the subject field. www.pooloflondon.com

For a complete list of Pool of London Press and Casemate titles, please contact:

CASEMATE PUBLISHERS (UK); Telephone (01865) 241249; Email: casemate-uk @casematepublishers.co.uk
www.casematepublishers.co.uk

CASEMATE PUBLISHERS (US) Telephone (610) 853-9131; Email: casemate @casematepublishing.com
www.casematepublishing.com

CONTENTS

INTRODUCTION

The Second World War had scarcely ended in 1945 before relations deteriorated between the Soviet Union, or Union of Soviet Socialist Republics (USSR), and the United States of America (USA), the two principal powers in the Allied coalition against Nazi Germany, first into mutual suspicion and then into a decades-long stand-off during which the slightest miscalculation could have plunged the world into a catastrophic nuclear conflict. This so-called Cold War was punctuated by a series of political crises between the USSR and USA, which had assumed the role of two superpowers leading mutually antagonistic military blocs in a deadly game of global domination, the one in the name of international communism, the other (at least notionally) in the defence of liberal democracy.

From the time of the Yalta Conference in 1945, at which the Western Allies in effect recognized a Soviet sphere of influence in eastern Europe that doomed the region to four decades of communist domination, to the collapse of those Soviet-backed regimes in 1989, Europe was at the epicentre of the Cold War. There were large-scale conflicts between the USA and revolutionaries in East Asia, in Korea and Vietnam, but these were not direct confrontations with the USSR, and only in Europe did the armed forces of the superpowers face each other directly across borders which had become so heavily militarized as to constitute, in the colourful phrase of Britain's wartime leader Winston Churchill, an "Iron Curtain".

After the Soviet Union detonated its first atomic bomb in 1949 and so joined the United States in the elite club of nuclear-armed countries, the superpowers knew that any war between them would be a nuclear one. In one sense this made war less likely – by the 1960s the American military doctrine was summed up in the foreboding phrase Mutual Assured Destruction, the likely outcome of any conflict. But the nuclear brinkmanship also made it more imperative for each superpower to understand the thinking of the other side, to squeeze out every last possible ounce of advantage in stealing its secrets, to spread confusion among its allies, and even to subvert its very system of government.

The Cold War thus became a golden age of espionage, with each side attempting to place agents in the other's countries, in particular in the opposing intelligence agency or in other positions where they might influence decision-makers, recruit further agents, or damage the enemy's interests through the theft of secrets, the spreading of disinformation or outright sabotage. In flashpoints such as West Berlin, a capitalist enclave within a communist sea, this secret struggle was particularly intense; at almost every corner, it sometimes seemed, a surveillance team lurked, tracking the movements of the other side.

Intelligence Agencies

The efforts of the contending powers in the Cold War's shadowy sister, the espionage wars, were co-ordinated by their respective intelligence agencies, most notably the Central Intelligence Agency (CIA) for the USA, MI6 for the United Kingdom (UK) and the KGB for the USSR. Most agencies had their roots in the Second World War (or even before it) or they were successors to organizations which had operated during that time. As such they initially used many techniques developed during the war and were staffed with officials whose careers had been shaped in the cauldron of global conflict (men such as Kim Philby, who betrayed British intelligence to the Soviets, saw "anti-Fascism" and the defence of international socialism as the primary cause rather than loyalty to the British state).

The CIA was established in 1947 to provide a source of intelligence to the US government independent of its military (and in the teeth of bitter opposition from the latter). Under the leadership of Director Allen Dulles (1953 to 1961), the agency grew into a leviathan, running covert operations worldwide. After intelligence failures (and a lack of political will) had failed to prevent the USSR's complete domination of postwar eastern Europe and its crushing of nationalist movements in Ukraine and the Baltic states (which were thoroughly penetrated by Soviet agents), the CIA's role in the overthrow of the Iranian premier Mohammed Mossadegh in 1953 and of the radical Guatemalan president Jacobo

Arbenz Guzmán in 1954 marked comparative triumphs. Disaster struck in May 1960 when a U-2 spy plane was shot down on a reconnaissance mission over the USSR, while a CIA-sponsored attempt to overthrow Cuba's communist leader, Fidel Castro, failed disastrously at the Bay of Pigs, irrevocably tarnishing the agency's image.

Throughout this period, and until the Cold War ended with the collapse of the Soviet Union in 1991, the CIA sparred with its Soviet counterpart the KGB (or *Komitet Gosudarstvennoy Bezopasnosti* – "Committee for State Security"), which was a comparative newcomer to the intelligence sphere, having been set up in 1954 as the successor to the NKVD, which had been Stalin's secret police and intelligence force. Unlike the CIA, which left domestic intelligence and counter-espionage operations to the Federal Bureau of Intelligence (FBI), the KGB operated at home and abroad. With functions including foreign intelligence collection and analysis, counter-intelligence, state security and monitoring of the population for signs of subversion or dissidence and the patrolling of the Soviet Union's borders, the KGB was the world's largest intelligence agency. Estimates of its staff reached as high as 130,000 at home, 250,000 abroad, and over a million informers within the Soviet Union. It ran a wide range of spy networks in the West, most notably in the USA, West Germany and the UK, some of which evaded detection for decades. An entire directorate of the KGB

Heel Bug

In the 1960s the StB (Czech intelligence service) installed a bug in the heel of the US ambassador's shoes while they were being repaired. The hidden microphone could be activated by the ambassador's butler, who just happened to be an StB agent.

Cuckoo Clock camera

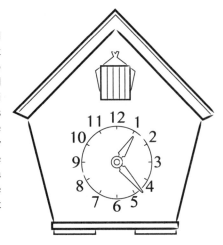

Intelligence services could conceal cameras in the most unusual objects. This cuckoo clock was specially modified by the East German Stasi by placing a camera lens in the opening above the 12 (which would normally house the "cuckoo"). The camera was operated by a cable inserted through the wall of the room where it was mounted.

(the Fifth) was devoted to keeping an eye on dissidents, and conducted surveillance against foreign embassies (and their agents, real or suspected). In one operation KGB-controlled workers laced the US Embassy with so many bugging devices during its rebuilding in the early 1980s, some of which were embedded in the concrete core of the new structure, that the new building was rendered unusable. The KGB also perfected the art of *dezinformatsya* ("disinformation"), by which it placed fabricated rumours in compliant (or unsuspecting) media outlets in a bid to discredit the USA and its allies. This extended to the forging in 1981 of a letter purporting to be from President Ronald Reagan to King Juan Carlos of Spain, imploring the latter to smooth the path to Spanish membership of NATO by "destroying the left-wing opposition".

Working alongside the KGB was the Chief Directorate of the General Staff (the *Glavnoye Razvedyvatelnoye Upravlenie* or GRU), the intelligence wing of the Soviet armed forces. Although its head was generally a former officer in the KGB, the GRU operated independently, concentrating on the acquisition of scientific secrets. The GRU initially recruited the FBI agent Robert Hanssen who spied for the Soviet Union and then Russia for 22 years until his arrest in 2001. The KGB was also assisted by intelligence agencies in the Soviet Union's satellite socialist countries, which were in general subordinate to its directions but some of which, such as East Germany's MfS

The "Thing"

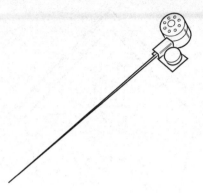

In the 1950s the Soviet government presented a wooden carving of the Great Seal of the United States to the American ambassador in Moscow. It hung for some time behind his desk, but turned out to contain a KGB listening device that relied on monitoring modulations to a radio wave caused by sound that struck a vibrating diaphragm in the device.

(*Ministerium für Staatssicherheit* or "Stasi") and Czechoslovakia's StB, ran autonomous and effective operations of their own.

In the UK espionage was split between a domestic agency, the Security Service or MI5, and the Secret Intelligence Service (SIS or MI6). Both had their origins in the Secret Service Bureau founded in 1909 and achieved their separate identities in the 1920s. Less flamboyant than the CIA, or inclined to extravagant attempts to destabilize entire regimes, MI6 was also hampered by a well-established Soviet spy network (the "Cambridge Spy Ring") that leaked massive quantities of high-grade intelligence back to the KGB in the 1940s and 1950s, while MI5, supposedly tasked with counter-espionage, was severely damaged by its failure to detect the Cambridge spies for almost 20 years.

Throughout the Cold War, espionage operations were principally directed through personnel embedded in embassies, working under diplomatic cover. The CIA and MI6 posts were generally called "stations", while those of the KGB (and GRU) were *Rezidentura*, with the head of the post referred to as the "Resident". In smaller posts there might be a handful of intelligence operatives, while in more sensitive locations they might even outnumber more conventional diplomatic staff. In 1971 British Prime Minister Edward Heath ordered the expulsion of 105 Soviet diplomats for spying, an indication of the enormous size of the USSR's espionage operations in the UK at the time. Even the smallest KGB *Rezidentura* had a dedicated cypher clerk to send encrypted telegrams back to Moscow (communications which were not seen by the regular diplomats or the ambassador, unless he happened to be a KGB operative). The larger *Rezidentura* had multiple officers running agents or "illegals", deep-cover operatives who had assumed a fake identity in order to live in the host country undetected, and technical experts who specialized in bugging devices and intercepting communications.

Throughout the Cold War agents were recruited by intelligence agencies in a number of ways. In Western countries the USSR had a ready supply of possible sympathizers in the local communist parties (there were 32,000 members in the USA in 1950). Some of these members either actively spied for the USSR, or acted as proxies for its intelligence services, recruiting agents who might believe (or convince themselves) that they were passing on secrets only to a sympathetic political party rather than to an enemy power. This fruitful area yielded agents such as Victor Perlo, a Marxist economist working in the US Treasury, who passed economic secrets to the USSR throughout the 1940s and who in addition ran a major network of Soviet spies in the USA. Others volunteered as "walk-ins", such as physicist Theodore Hall, who leaked information about the Manhattan Project to develop a nuclear bomb (but who was never prosecuted). Because communist sympathizers were relatively easy for the FBI to track, the *Rezidentura* in Western countries also employed "illegals" such as Gordon Lonsdale, aka Konon Molody, a commissioned Soviet naval officer who assumed the identity of a dead Canadian. Lonsdale/Molody operated in the USA in the 1950s under the direction of Rudolf Abel (an illegal whose real name was Alexander Belov), before travelling to the UK in 1955. There he established a business as a salesman of jukeboxes, a cover that meant he travelled without arousing suspicion and was able to act as handler to the Portland spy ring, a group of Admiralty officials who handed over secrets from the Underwater Weapons Establishment at Portland.

Defectors

The level of surveillance in communist countries made life rather more complicated for the CIA and MI6 officers trying to operate there. Unsanctioned contacts between Eastern bloc citizens and foreign diplomats would be rapidly reported back to the intelligence agencies, leading to the arrest of the would-be informant and possibly expulsion for the diplomats. Western intelligence agencies were therefore disproportionately reliant on defectors, trained intelligence agents, military officials or diplomatic personnel who came to them offering secrets in exchange for a new life in the West (although occasionally they remained in post as "defectors in place", running the terrible risk of detection and execution). Gordon Lonsdale was detected after Michael Golienewski, a Polish intelligence officer (who was also acting as a KGB agent), defected to the CIA in West Berlin, bringing with him hundreds of rolls of film of classified documents.

Defections sometimes came from the heart of the Soviet intelligence establishment. Oleg Penkovsky, a GRU officer who had served – as most senior GRU personnel did – as a military attaché, had access to critical secrets, particularly concerning rocket and missile technology and strategy. The indirect approach forced on would-be defectors in the USSR meant Penkovsky tried to get in contact with the US Embassy by handing a letter to American tourists in August 1960, but was initially treated as a possible agent provocateur. In the end MI6 and the CIA shared him as a source, providing him with miniature cameras to photograph sensitive documents, which he provided in such abundance that it required a team of 20 analysts to comb through it all. So dangerous for spies was the Moscow environment that Penkovsky rejected "dead drops", the classic method of exchanging information with controllers (in which documents are hidden in an innocuous location, such as under a rock or taped beneath a bridge and the spy's handlers are alerted to check it by a separate signal, such as a chalk mark on a lamppost). Instead he handed over rolls of film (to the wife of an MI6 officer at the British Embassy) by "brush contact", a sleight-of-hand manoeuvre to pass on items during a close, and seemingly innocent, approach in a park (often while she was walking with her children). Penkovsky provided invaluable information to the USA during the Cuban Missile Crisis, when his intelligence may have given President Kennedy and his team a crucial edge in facing down Khrushchev. In the end Penkovsky was detected quite by chance when a separate security scare caused the KGB to conduct blanket surveillance of the US and British embassies for several weeks each year; as a result the team tailing his MI6 contact saw her make a brush contact with an unidentified Russian. It did not take long to confirm that this was Penkovsky, but to be doubly sure the KGB smeared a

toxic substance on his office chair which resulted in his being hospital-
ized for several days, giving agents ample time to gain access to, and
bug, his home and gain reams of incriminating evidence.

Among the most valuable intelligence a defector brought led
to the unmasking of networks of enemy agents in his new host
country. One of the first post-war defectors was Igor Gouzenko, a
cypher clerk in the Soviet Embassy in Ottawa, who made his move
in 1945. Naively unsure of how to go about betrayal, Gouzenko,
with a cache of secret documents to prove his worth, first tried to
defect at the offices of the *Ottawa Journal*. Rebuffed, he offered his
services to the Royal Canadian Mounted Police, followed by the
Ministry of Justice, both of which also turned him away. Only the in-
tervention of one of Gouzenko's neighbours, who happened to be
a sergeant in the Royal Canadian Air Force, smoothed the way to
the hapless Russian handing himself over to Canadian intelligence.
The documents he brought not only compromised a Soviet spy
network in Canada, but also for the first time revealed an extensive
web of Soviet espionage aimed at stealing atomic secrets from the
USA. His information led to the arrest of Allan Nunn May, a British
physicist who had reported to the KGB on the nuclear tests at Los
Alamos and had handed the Soviets samples of the Uranium-235
used in the first American atom bomb.

Step by step the Soviet spy ring unravelled, aided by the breaking
in 1946 of the cypher used by their handlers in the USA to communicate with Moscow. Code-named Venona, news of the USA's
ability to read these messages was so sensitive that it was not officially
acknowledged until the 1990s. One such decrypted message led the
USA to the German-born physicist Klaus Fuchs who had been passing information on the development of an atom bomb since 1941
and who rose to be the head of the theoretical physics division at
Britain's atomic energy establishment at Harwell. Fuchs was arrested
in late 1949 and confessed to MI5, leading to the detention of the
rest of the ring, which included Harry Gold, who had been Fuchs's
courier, and Julius and Ethel Rosenberg, who had played a key role
in co-ordinating the network and suffered the severest penalty when
they were executed in 1953.

Although an opportune defection, assiduous signals intelligence
work, brilliant code-breaking, and old-fashioned analysis and tradecraft

had blown apart the key Soviet network in the USA, things might have been worse but for the existence of a network of "defectors in place" working for the USSR. Later known as the "Cambridge Spy Ring", as its members had been recruited by the NKVD at Cambridge University in the 1930s, its key operatives were Kim Philby, who worked in MI6 from 1941, and Guy Burgess, who was first an MI6 officer before transferring to the Foreign Office in 1944. This included a stint from 1950 at the British Embassy in Washington, which put him (and Philby who was the embassy's MI6 liaison officer with the CIA and FBI) in a unique position to hand secret information to their Soviet masters. Preceding them in Washington was Donald Maclean, another diplomat-turned-defector, who became head of the Foreign Office's American Department. For years the three were able to frustrate any internal investigation or external scrutiny of Soviet moles in British intelligence. To take just one example, in August 1945 the Soviet vice-consul in Istanbul, Konstanin Volkov, who in fact worked for the NKVD, contacted his British opposite number offering to defect, with the lure that he would name over 300 Soviet agents in Turkey and 250 in Britain. On the latter list the names of Philby, Burgess and Maclean (as well as Anthony Blunt and other members of the ring) would doubtless have figured. Philby managed to engineer his appointment as the MI6 officer sent to Istanbul to negotiate the defection and promptly betrayed the affair to his handlers, with the result that Volkov was spirited back to Moscow and executed.

The Cambridge spies were finally caught as a result of a Venona decrypt indicating that a Soviet spy code-named Homer might just be Maclean. On 25 May 1951 he and Burgess fled to Moscow by a circuitous route. Somehow Philby, despite a multitude of incriminating circumstantial evidence, weathered the storm, only finally defecting in 1963 when renewed suspicions threatened his belated arrest.

About this Book

Intelligence agencies, both Western and in Russia, the successor state to the USSR, have been understandably reluctant to cast too much light on their Cold War operations and have controlled the flow of information which has emerged. Whereas espionage and subversion operations during the Second World War are comparatively well documented, those which took place during the Cold War are still, at best, only partly understood and, at worst, remain almost totally obscure. The CIA has released a number of documents, but these generally deal with policy rather than operational details, while MI5 and MI6 have taken the view that while material from the Second World War and before it may gradually be allowed into the public domain, the Cold War remains off-limits. Paradoxically for a tightly controlled society, material relating to the KGB and GRU is more abundant, in large part because for a period in the 1990s the Soviet intelligence archives opened their doors to Western researchers in the hope of retaining relevance (and gaining hard currency).

Although there is an abundant literature on Cold War espionage, much of it relies on the interpretation of hints, the filtration of disinformation from selective leaks and a dose of guesswork. Added to this are the precious accounts of defectors themselves, but when reading these there is always the question of whether the accounts are self-serving, exaggerating the agents' importance in the hope of receiving better treatment from their new masters, or perhaps designed to cast their old employers in the worst possible light. In a world of paranoia and smoke and mirrors some of the best hints of espionage practise might even be found in the milieu of the spy novels and films which, safely labelled as fiction, have proliferated since the 1940s.

The documents in this book represent part of the small core of hard information around which the rest of the story of Cold War espionage must be woven. They include a manual of secret recognition signs for spies written by a stage magician for the CIA, a lecture instructing "illegals" in the USA how to conduct themselves without being detected, a dossier on British interrogation techniques and the real protocols for handling a dead drop by the Soviet defector Penkovsky. A compelling account of a real-life defection by a Soviet GRU operative in Teheran sits alongside telegrams that almost sparked a nuclear conflict. They represent merely the tip of the iceberg of briefings, counter-briefings, instructions and orders which issued from the KGB, CIA and MI6, but together they shed an invaluable light on the dark world of the Cold War spies.

CHAPTER 1

OPERATIONAL TRAINING AND TECHNIQUES

Camp 020 – A Digest of Ham

Although the political roots of the Cold War are to be found in the later part of the Second World War, many of the espionage techniques and organizations that characterized it were developed in the early 1940s.

Following the Axis advance across Europe in 1940, and the very real threat of an invasion of Britain, there was an upsurge in German attempts to infiltrate spies into the country. These would-be agents often posed as one of the thousands of refugees fleeing Nazi occupation. The first obstacle they faced was the London Reception Centre near Clapham Junction, established to process the refugees and identify those whose cover stories did not pass scrutiny. Anyone who failed this initial vetting was passed on to Camp 020, set up by MI5 in July 1940 in a house near Ham Common in Richmond as an interrogation centre for enemy spies. Its commandant, Lieutenant-Colonel Robert "Tin Eye" Stephens (who acquired his unusual nickname from the thick monocle he habitually wore), was a formidable, idiosyncratic character who soon overcame the problems posed by the lack of a pool of trained interrogators.

The techniques he devised were detailed in a *A Digest of Ham*, a secret MI5 history of Camp 020, written after the war to aid future counter-espionage efforts. Stephens rejected the crude use of violence in favour of more subtle psychological techniques aimed at wearing down, confusing and ultimately "breaking" the prisoner. Although the ultimate threat of execution remained (Stephens remarked that "figuratively, a spy in war should be at the point of a bayonet"), his panels of interrogating officers employed stool pigeons, "sympathy men" and even bugging devices to elicit information which could crack the agent's resistance. The ultimate prize was to turn them into double agents feeding back disinformation to Berlin through the "Double Cross" system. If all else failed, the threat of transferring the prisoner to "Cell Fourteen", a holding cell in which the spies had been led to believe – quite wrongly – that the most appalling tortures would be inflicted on them, broke all but the most recalcitrant.

At the end of the war, Stephens was posted to a new detention centre at Bad Nenndorff in occupied Germany. Many senior Nazis were interrogated, but within a year the profile of the camp's "clients" changed and the first Soviet agents were detained there.

CAMP 020 – A DIGEST OF HAM

On the Interrogation of Spies

1. The Network of Investigation

Interrogation is only a part of a pattern. It may be the foreground, it may hold the highlight of a jigsaw picture, but all said and done it is only a part of the whole.

It is the inexperienced interrogator who arrogates to himself credit for a break or credit for a completed report. It is the Intelligence Officer of sense and experience who insists upon assistance from every conceivable source before he starts his battle.

A spy is picked up through a trace, an intercept, a mistake on the part of the spy himself, through the work of an agent-double, the treachery of a fellow-spy; through these and many other means well known to M.I.5. Early information is in a Special Registry.

There are documents on the spy himself; there is the possibility of real evidence such as secret ink concealed in his clothes. There is the man who can fit one piece of information into another and give it meaning. Early information is passed to the Central Registry, and the bells start ringing all over again.

Only a novice will plunge into an interrogation unarmed. His action is as fantastic as a man who would play bridge with the dummy face down. He finesses for a card which is already in his possession. ...

2. On the Conduct of a C.I. Investigation

(a) Preliminaries

The penalty for espionage is death. If the spy tells the truth he may live. There is no guarantee; it is a hope, not more.

The quicker the spy realises that fundamental position the better. Psychology and discipline should produce that result.

Arrest must be efficient. The less said the better. The quicker the handcuffs are slipped on the more pronounced is the effect of stark reality. The quicker ill fitting and shabby prison garb take the place of sartorial elegance the more profound and depressing is the effect.

No exceptions. No chivalry. No gossip. No cigarettes.

Incommunicado is the watchword.

The remaining preliminaries are all calculated to maintain discipline and to reduce the morale of the spy. Rules must be framed and rigidly observed. Otherwise, in the urgency, in the excitement of the moment, some vital clue, some obvious precaution will be overlooked.

Take property as an example. Property must be removed, sorted, listed. A meticulous search of the body and of clothing must follow. Nikolai HANSEN had secret ink in the cavity of a tooth. HIMMLER had cyanide in his mouth; GOERING kept his poison in his navel for over a year. Cotton, impregnated with secret ink, has been threaded into the collar stuffing of a coat. A full-stop in a love letter may mean much. GILINSKY slipped Security at Trinidad and Customs in England with 40,000 dollars by the means, old-age, of a false bottom to the drawer of a trunk. BLAY Pigrau had a password in the fly-buttons of his trousers. Take documents as another example. Passports and identity papers must be checked for forgery before interrogation, even if there is no time for immediate examination by violet ray. All names and addresses whatever in letters, papers or notebooks should be seen by the local registry before interrogation and there should be no delay in forwarding them to the Central Registry for conclusive check.

Odd notes, even hieroglyphs, demand intelligent study. A trivial entry in one page of a notebook coupled with another in a distant page may well be the key to a code; and if it is discovered, it is at once a trump card for a break. ...

(b) The Plan

Since it is team work that counts, there must be a plan, clear and definite, understood by everyone concerned. Admittedly it must be flexible, admittedly it may have to be changed; but the responsibility is from first to last in the Commandant. A precious interrogator, a secretive soul, or a poseur is an outstanding menace. The ideal arrangement is for a Commandant to interrogate with the whole weight of his establishment in support. Various factors militate against this system, but in a crucial case it is well worth while to call a halt to all other activities until the case is broken. It is the attack in maximum force at the critical moment that is decisive.

(c) The First Vital Interview

A board of officers is appointed. The atmosphere is that of a General Court Martial.

One officer interrogates. In no circumstances whatsoever may he be interrupted. Unless he issues an invitation, no other officer may put any question whatever.

In urgent cases two officers alternately take summaries. The summary progresses by shifts in an adjoining office. A quick report should be available for a D.R. within an hour of completion of the interrogation.

The interpreter sits next to the interrogator. Unless other facilities exist a stenographer is present and is relieved unobtrusively every half hour.

An officer may be required as property master. Instant production of any item of evidence is his duty.

The prisoner is marched in and remains standing to attention throughout the proceedings. No liberties, no interruptions, no gesticulations. He speaks when he is spoken to. He answers the questions; no more, no less.

Studious politeness, the courtesy of a chair, the friendliness of a cigarette, these things breed familiarity and confidence in a spy. Figuratively, a spy in war should be at the point of a bayonet.

It is prudent to fix identity at an early stage in the proceedings. If it is difficult to get specific information as to the real identity of persons such as STALIN, MOLOTOV and TITO, because of their political aliases, how much more necessary is it to obtain it in relation to a spy because of his underground activities?

Early in the war one young officer thought he knew much. Somewhat myopic in vision, he relied upon academic training. He disapproved of a break. He marshaled his facts. He set out some three hundred questions. He gave the spy the benefit of the case against him. Courteously he invited him to react. With equal courtesy came back the answer:-

"Sir, I regret I am not Mr X."
"Ah – so none of my questions apply."
"Sir, that is so."

The officer reported back it was a case of mistaken identity. He was wrong again. But the spy knew the case against him; he knew also the gaps. It took a month of Sundays to break the man; few of the gaps were ever filled.

What is the secret of success in interrogation? Firstly, perhaps, the knowledge, it may be as slender as an intuition, that the man is a spy. Secondly, the motive which drove the man into espionage. Given a shred of evidence, the rest is a matter for personality and experience; and an interrogator should be ashamed of himself if he fails.

What should be the attitude of the interrogator? The bitter, un-compromising approach is as effective as any. And as with a man, so with a women – no quarter. And often how profitable, the instant there is a glimmering of an admission, to make the man write it down. Still standing, he can write down the second admission, and the third, until the cumulative effect undermines his morale. How easy to wriggle out of a verbal lapse; how difficult to erase a written admission? Such admissions, one after another, are the milestones on the road to surrender. Pressure must be maintained.

Pressure is attained by personality, tone, and rapidity of question; insistence upon an immediate answer, recapitulation. The requirement is a driving attack in the nature of a blast which will scare a man out of his wits.

Again, as with a man, so with a woman. There is no room for chivalry in modern espionage.

Never promise, never bargain. The man's neck is in your grasp. Never forget it; never let him forget it.

Never strike a man. For one thing it is the act of a coward. For another, it is unintelligent, for the spy will give an answer to please, an answer to escape punishment. And having given a false answer, all else depends upon the false premise.

Break off when a confession in writing has been obtained. Set the prisoner further questions, against time, in his cell. Send for him again, whatever the hour of the night, and continue until the goal is achieved. Blow hot, blow cold. No respite, no time to recover, no time to plan.

Mental hell. Worn out, dispirited, dejected, a time will come when there is absolute surrender. The man can stand the strain no longer.

The strain upon the interrogator is equal if not greater. The difference? Why, the interrogator is free, and the spy is condemned. The interrogator can celebrate; the spy can console himself in solitary confinement with his failure.

But this is the bright side of the picture. If the interrogator fails during the first vital hours, trouble untold is in store. And each interrogator of experience has tasted the bitter dregs of disappointment. Probably he is a better man for it.

3. On Special Devices

… (b) The Stool Pigeon

Vitriol is an indifferent medium in which to portray a stool pigeon in any land whatever. Essentially he is a despicable character, treacherous to a degree, mistrusted by both sides, and a lasting anxiety to any administration. To call a man a spitzel, a cimbel, lokduif or a mouchoir, is worse than the casting of doubt upon the parentage of a man down Silvertown way.

Risks abound. The introduction of a stool pigeon is a crude device against which a spy is warned during his elementary training. It follows that the stool pigeon, ab initio, is suspect. Equally does it follow on the other side that everything said by this man of treachery must be subject to cover or independent corroboration, preferably both. Then when the stool pigeon fails, as almost invariably he does fail, the interrogator earns the contempt of the spy, the investigation is irretrievably lost, the man himself is blown to the rest of the prison, and an overall reticence may well affect other cases under inquiry. Next, equity is such that the gallant gentleman cannot be punished for his original espionage crime for the very good reason that the prosecution themselves do not come to court with clean hands. The consequence is that the man becomes body nuisance number one in an espionage prison for months, maybe for years. In the ultimate, when the war is over, the stool pigeon blackmails the Secret Service concerned into the grant of his freedom, a pension, and ever increasing increments thereto. In circumstances such as these, it is perhaps not overstressing the case to suggest that creatures of this kidney should only be used as a last resort.

Two cases fall outside this melancholy conclusion. First there is the man who is not, properly speaking, a stool pigeon at all; rather is he the trained agent introduced to act that part. Great must be his histrionic and linguistic ability; infinite must be the patience in priming him for his part. Clearly, he must be a first class secret service agent, an individual found, perhaps, once in a generation. The second type, equally rare and no less gifted, is the stool pigeon freak who responds to training, subtle handling, who proceeds without brief, and gives no information at all. He is an instrument of psychology. The Belgian, HUYSMANS, was an outstanding example during the War. He was promised nothing, nothing at all. His only glimmer of hope was to save his life, to save the life of his wife. Himself arrested in Lisbon and sent to England, capital was made of the fortunate circumstance that his wife followed in another plane. HUYSMANS was told the British could snatch her from the clutches of the Germans. In due course, she was prevailed upon to write to him from Holloway Gaol. The omniscience and power of the Secret Service were thus proved. HUYSMANS was permitted occasionally to meet prisoners. He did not know what their cases were about. Quite simply he gave advice. Because of his worldly experience he carried conviction; because of his genuine ignorance of the cases he carried sincerity. First he would tell his own story, rich in detail, essentially true. Then he would dilate upon the strange power of the British Secret Service; he could quote the incident of his wife. He would talk of the fairness of British methods. Sorrowfully he would depart and remain away until the spy himself asked to see him again. That too, had to be finessed and sometimes adroitly refused by the Authorities themselves who hoped against hope the request would be repeated.

Then followed HUYSMANS second approach:- "I do not wish to listen to your story; I have too much trouble of my own. All I can say for myself is that I am alive."

Further urged by a desperate spy to help he would refuse again:- "The responsibility is too great. All I can say is that I spoke the truth, they checked every word of it – and I am alive."

Later, perhaps, the odd message would be delivered:- "Number X is, I think, ready to talk. Perhaps he will react to sympathy, this one, rather than to heavy interrogation. It is for you, honoured Sir, to decide. I do not know his case."

In retrospect, HUYSMANS is one of the most fascinating espionage studies of the war. But desperate was the anxiety. Every move was planned, words weighed, cover kept; we were never suspected. Essentially he had one master only; obviously he was sparingly used.

In the ultimate, freedom was HUYSMANS' reward. Maybe he will carry an uneasy feeling to his grave, that he is still being watched.

(c) The Cross-Ruff

The Cross-ruff is a process which can be effectively used in the case of joint spies. Since their cover story is common they tend to work in concert. There is a pact to keep silence. If one breaks, however, in interrogation the other usually follows suit. Segregation is the first essential and extremely heavy interrogation of the weaker character then follows. If successful the results are reduced to writing and the principal is then faced with the defection of his comrade. Usually he is intelligent enough to appreciate the hopelessness of the position and surrender.

One case is that of Joseph and Mathilde GOBIN. The covering report of 19 January 1945 set out in the second part of this paper sufficiently sets out the facts.

A second case is that of the Icelanders FRESENIUS, BJORNSSON and JULIUSSON. FRESENIUS was the master while the other two were no more than his servants. They were kept separate, and to reverse a phrase, the lead was taken through weakness into strength. First a partial break was obtained from BJORNSSON. This resulted in a limited admission from JULIUSSON. JULIUSSON was played against BJORNSSON and vice versa. The result was an accurate background of the whole mission, and FRESENIUS, the master, was then attacked with much success.

The outstanding feature of this very important operational case at the time of "D" Day is that the bulk of the information was obtained within 48 hours.

(d) Confrontation

Confrontation, in theory, seems such an obvious and effective weapon. In practice, it is a most dangerous expedient which may well ruin the whole course of an investigation.

One case in point is that of VERLINDEN and LAUREYSSENS.

VERLINDEN was the informer; he was trustworthy; his evidence against LAUREYSSENS was damning to a degree. VERLINDEN, [...] had actually introduced LAUREYSSENS to the German spy master, HOFFMAN. He had provided accommodation for LAUREYSSENS. He exposed the details of the mission. He described how LAUREYSSENS had earned his keep in LISBON by pin pointing targets and AA defences in SWANSEA. LAUREYSSENS admitted the contacts, but swore they were purely social. Nothing would move him. Confrontation was the only solution. VERLINDEN told his story with obvious sincerity. LAUREYSSENS with impressive calm, looked VERLINDEN straight in the face and denied all knowledge of him whatever.

Another case was that of EDVARDSEN, DE DEEKER, Vera ERICHSEN and WAELTI. Here EDVARDSEN told his story with obvious conviction. Against DE DEEKER and WAELTI complete failure must be recorded: WAELTI denied ever having set eyes on him before and DE DEEKER (though he admitted having under-

stood EDVARDSEN's story which was told throughout in English)
contented himself with the ironical comment that the gentleman's
memory was too good and he appeared to have got the story off by
heart.

This failure was redeemed in part by success against Vera
ERICHSEN. She did in fact retract some previous information and
substitute new detail which certainly discomfited DE DEEKER and
WAELTI in turn.

If resort is had to confrontation obvious precautions must be
taken. The interrogator must be certain the informer will give his
evidence at the critical time; he must ensure that only relevant information is given.

When confrontation is complete, argument and questions must
be prohibited. Finally there must be a definite plan to meet either
success or failure.

Failure in such cases is complete and utter, and an interrogator
who has not anticipated the contingency is a novice indeed.

… (f) The Legend of Cell Fourteen

"You will now be sent to Cell Fourteen.

"In time of peace it was a padded cell, so protected that raving
maniacs could not bash out their brains against the wall. Some recovered. Some committed suicide. Some died from natural causes.

"The mortuary is conveniently opposite.

"In time of war accommodation is short. Cell Fourteen is no
longer a padded cell. Now there is little difference between that cell
and any other cell. Perhaps it is remote, and cold and a little dark.
That is all. But for some reason the sinister reputation persists.

"Some spies believe in the supernatural. They say certain psychic
elements are present. Some spies suffer from claustrophobia. Some
spies have a guilty conscience and know no peace.

"Results are interesting. Some spies have told the truth and have
been transferred. Some have committed suicide. Some have passed
out for the last time to their judicial hanging – their rich desert.

"I shall not see you again. I do not know how long you will be
there. Petitions will be ignored. Only if you decide to tell the truth
will you be allowed to write.

"But just remember this, that we are winning the war in spite of you – one man only – in captivity. Maybe you are holding back information which is already in our possession. Maybe you are more of a fool than a hero.

"For the rest, you will be interested perhaps in the movements of the sentry who will cover you each quarter of the hour. Perhaps he comes to check. Perhaps he comes with food. Perhaps he comes – to take you away – for the last time."

At first sight that address is sheer unadulterated melodrama. But the fact remains that it proved successful on many occasions during the war. Much depended upon delivery, atmosphere, timing – last but not least upon the personality of the interrogator.

To use a phrase hackneyed in melodrama – it's not so much what you say but the way that you say it.

Effects varied. A German lost his arrogance. A Spaniard lost the glint of his dark and fiery eye. An Egyptian visibly wasted. An Italian gesticulated wildly for writing materials within the hour. A Frenchman lost his nerve and talked of the "cellule des condamnés." An Icelander remained unmoved; between Cell Fourteen and the land of desolation there was no contrast.

Danger lay in the finality of Cell Fourteen. If it failed, then little hope remained of a break.

The lesson of Cell Fourteen lay in the exploitation of a trivial circumstance, the existence of an old padded cell. The Intelligence officer responsible asked himself this question: "If I were a captured spy, what would I hate most in my predicament?"

Thereafter it became a matter of psychology – to say what would hurt the mind most.

(g) The Technique of "Blow Hot-Blow Cold"

Some spies have diplomatic cover, they have grandiose delusions, they are always on their dignity. Fortunately, in war, liberties can be taken. The diplomat is reduced to the state of a common prisoner. He wears ill fitting prison clothes and there is nothing more disconcerting to a poseur than to relieve him of his pince-nez, his false teeth and his bootlaces. The grounds are humanitarian – in case the prisoner feels impelled to commit suicide.

Then the stage is set. The diplomat is brought before the interrogation board. He is subjected to a withering fire of invective. One of the officers attempts to intervene and is sourly rebuked. One or two unimportant mistakes of fact are made. The man is then summarily removed without an opportunity of saying a word for himself.

His indignation is intense, but so also is his fear.

Then, by chance, the officer who intervened on his behalf, is the orderly officer of the day. He treats the diplomat with courtesy; a link is established. The Commandant is an unreasonable man. The process of investigation, however, is inexorable. Much is known of the diplomat; the Commandant intends to get the rest from him. He does not appreciate sensitive people, he treats all spies alike. He is a hard man. He know no mercy.

Perhaps the officer could smoothe the way to a dignified statement of fact? Perhaps further painful scenes, such as that of the morning, can be avoided? Perhaps the diplomat and his family can be saved from the terrors of blackmail?

"Sleep well, and if you would like writing materials, or if you want my assistance, I will come. I will try to help you."

The scheme and variations of it succeeded in a number of cases. The officer who had acted like a snake in the grass was usually regarded as an "English Gentleman" while the Commandant had the invidious distinction of being likened to HEYDRICH.

(h) The Cover Story

The cover story is the protective armour of the spy; that manufactured by the Germans had many chinks.

To be effective a spy must live his cover story. If he professes to a knowledge of Liverpool he must know the way to the Adelphi; if he claims familiarity with Brighton he must know something of grotesque in the Regency quarter. In London he must know something of the rivers, the Underground, the sparkling and the shabby hotels.

And so in reverse, the interrogator must live the cover story with the spy. If he has not been there, he must toil through the maps, the tourist guide books and the photographs available. Endless, driving questioning on detail may result in that very pleasant moment "You lie – you have never been there."

Sometimes an astute spy will make a partial confession and set out the rest of his activities in a plausible tale. HANSEN landed in England by parachute. He immediately admitted to a W/T set. What more could a novice interrogator require? Here was an honest man, a man who hated the Germans. But somehow it all sounded too plausible. Perseverance resulted in a remarkable cover story. HANSEN was to be very candid, if caught. No doubt he would get his release. Then he could return to the scene of the drop, for it was there that he had concealed a second W/T set which he could operate at leisure under little suspicion.

(i) "Sympathy Men"[+]

"Sympathy Men" were used to a considerable extent by the Germans during the war and to a limited extent by ourselves. Their role was to gain the confidence of PW by expressing sympathy with their lot (a good opening was to pretend to have been a PW oneself in the 1914–18 war) and, in the guise of welfare officers, to provide PW with cigarettes and other comforts, this being done allegedly against camp regulations. The "Sympathy Man" thus gained the reputation of being a man who could be trusted and could then try to obtain information, sometimes by using the "BF approach", eg by asking a U-boat rating infantile questions about submarines and gradually leading up to some technical point which it had not been possible to elucidate by direct interrogation or via "M".[++] In other cases the "Sympathy Man", without actually asking questions, would try to get the PWs' minds on to a certain topic and then leave the cell, hoping that the "M" reaction would obtain the desired information.

… (k) Faking of Newspapers

"By arrangement with one of the newspapers, a few copies of a daily newspaper would be printed containing a spoof article in place of one of the same length which had appeared in the normal

---

[+] An officer of M.I.9 writes on items (i) to (m) as they are applicable more to Prisoners of War than Spies. [++] "M" indicates a secret recording device.

edition. These copies would then be given to selected PW and "M" would keep watch. A successful instance of this occurred in late 1941, when two U-boat officers were given a paper containing an alleged Admiralty communiqué giving the numbers and commandant's names of U-boats sunk to date, some of the numbers and names being intentionally wrong. In due course the officers came across the paragraph, discussed it eagerly and laughed at the mistakes; this put them on the right path and the eventual "M" report gave an almost complete picture of what U-boats and commanders were still operating at that time."

There can be no standard form as every espionage case has its individual characteristics. There are, however, certain underlying principles. Furthermore a standard framework is worth consideration so long as it is not used for slavish interpretation.

Underlying principles are as follows:-

(i) A short report in time is worth an encyclopaedia out of date.

(ii) Fact, and fact only, must appear in the report.
"On the one hand the spy may, mean .....
On the other hand the real fact is probably ....."
How many times has this gibberish been seen?
A report containing that sort of thing must be thrown out at once. In terms the interrogator has not done his job.

(iii) The proper place for opinion, interpretation and a call for action is in a covering memorandum.

(iv) There is no room in any report for a percentage assessment of reliability.

(v) Sentences must be short and to the point – Gibbon is dead.

Official CIA Manual of Trickery and Deception

As the Cold War progressed, the CIA turned to unconventional techniques to gain an edge against their KGB counterparts (whose successful exploits including an assassination using a gas gun hidden in rolled-up newspapers). In 1953 the Agency established MKULTRA, a programme which encompassed almost 150 projects, including experiments on the effect of drugs, notably LSD, and their possible use as weapons. Among the unusual results of the MKULTRA programme were a toothpaste tube that shot a .22 calibre round and a range of creative ideas for the assassination of Fidel Castro, many of which focused on the Cuban communist leader's penchant for cigars, and included lacing them with a hallucinogen, concealing explosives inside them and treating them with a depilator that was supposed to cause his famed beard to fall out.

One of MKULTRA's less outlandish projects was the commissioning in 1953 of a training manual from John Mulholland, a renowned stage magician, who was enticed from his position as editor of *The Sphinx,* America's leading magic publication, to work for the CIA. Mulholland deployed his mastery of the magician's stagecraft to compile a wealth of tips on places of concealments (such as secret pockets and women's high heels), and on ways to seem inconspicuous so that the agent could hide "in clear sight". He also produced a shorter guide on "Recognition Signals" by which agents could safely recognize each other. From the relatively mundane, such as the use of different coloured button-holes, to the rather less obvious varying of tie knots and colours and the genuinely bizarre employment of different shoe-lace patterns to convey a hidden message, Mulholland provided agents with a huge repertoire of concealed signals.

Mulholland's work was ordered destroyed, alongside most of the MKULTRA programme's records, in 1973, but a single copy somehow survived as a testament to Cold War agent spycraft.

OFFICIAL CIA MANUAL OF TRICKERY AND DECEPTION

Recognition Signals

The problem is that A and B, who have to work together, do not know or have descriptions for recognizing one another. A variation of the problem is that only one knows the other.

The problem is involved because of the many conditions which must be considered. It is possible that A and B may be able to meet and converse. It also is quite possible that it is advisable never to meet. A may be of a totally different social stratum (by role or fact), so that there would be few places both A and B could go. It might be that because of the job of one (such as a waiter), it would be either easy or impossible to have the meeting or identification take place at the job locale. Many jobs would materially limit the hours during which the worker could absent himself so as to be at another location.

Other conditions also must be considered. Were A to arrive at an airport, train, or bus station, it might be necessary for B to be able at a distance, and instantly, to recognize A. This would require some sign or signal visible at a distance and yet not noticeable to the uninformed. Almost the same conditions would apply were A and B to pass one another on the street or in a square or public park.

Other signs and signals might be better were the contact to be made in a lobby of a business building, in a museum, gallery, or library. Still other means of identification might serve were the meeting in a restaurant, bar, or store. Of course, no clothing variations could be used were the meeting between two bathers at a public beach.

In each of these situations, and others which may come to mind, it will be remembered that while A must recognize B, it also is necessary for B to identify A. And each must have a way of knowing that the other has made the identification.

Because the problem has so many variations, it is obvious that there must be different means of identification available to meet the different conditions.

The most obvious signaling device may be called "The Chrysanthemum in the Buttonhole Technique." Naturally, such a boutonniere would rarely be suitable, but it exemplifies the qualifications such a signaling device should have. First, a flower in the buttonhole is not an unusual practice of men everywhere. Second, it can be seen instantly. Third, it has color and color attracts attention. An alternate to color is differentiation in size. (A chrysanthemum certainly is larger than any flower normally worn.) Fourth, of itself the wearing of a flower is meaningless. (However, in the case of flowers, any specific flower lacks the basic qualification of availability anywhere and at any season of the year.)

It would seem best to divide methods for signaling into two classifications: those to be used at a distance and those for close-up use. Whereas every method which occurs to this writer for distance might also be used for close-up as well, there are a number of close-up methods which have a subtlety that makes them admirable for this purpose and they could serve a wider range of uses than most distance methods.

For distance signaling (other than manual) are variations in attire. These must be both permissible so as not to attract attention and yet clearly visible at a distance to the knowing observer. A varicolored feather in a hatband is such a device. Such feathers are generally worn and the visible, but not noticeable, distinction would be in the combination of colors used. A necktie made of material of a particular shade, or having a combination of unusual colors, might be used. Tying a tie (either four-in-hand or bow) with an unusual knot cannot be seen at a distance but can be used closeup. A twist in a knot is easily seen by anyone looking for it and is unlikely to be observed by anyone else. Even when it is noticed, it is ascribed to error rather than intent. Variations in the bow of a hatband also are easy to make and will pass unnoticed by anyone not especially looking for it. Here again, however, the change in the bow cannot be seen at a great distance.

Carrying a parcel which is, to use the retail store's term, "gift wrapped" can be seen at a distance. The special paper and/or the color of the ribbon or string can be seen at an amazing distance. Naturally, the situation would have to be such that carrying a gift would be natural and there would have to be a gift in the package on the chance that it would be opened. Instead of gift wrapping the parcel, ordinary paper could be used and the paper held closed by several wide colored rubber bands. Or the rubber bands could be put around the package in a prescribed manner. Instead of a package, a book might be used and held closed by the rubber bands. Another way of using a book would be to have it covered with a protective paper, as is commonly done with schoolbooks.

Ink (invisible except when special colored glasses are used) on packages, book wrappers, or baggage labels can be seen at a distance. The special value of such ink is that added information can be given by writing a large code letter or number.

Court plaster, surgeon's tape, Band-Aids, or any similar covering for cuts makes an excellent signaling device. It may be used on the face at any spot where one might cut himself shaving, or on almost any part of the hands, or, when in swimming, on an ankle or foot. The location of the tape, its size, and its shape all may be used to modify the signal, or to make it more definite that it is a signal. In some instances, it may well be necessary to have the tape cover an actual cut in the flesh. Except for that one point, the method has every advantage possible and is useful at a distance and close up.

While some of the following signals also can be used for considerable distance, most are for nearby use.

It might be well to point out that the absence of something often is as usable a signal as can be found. A missing vest or sleeve button, a shoelace missing in a workingman's shoe, or dissimilar laces, the absence of a bow on the ribbon of a hat, a strap at only one end of a suitcase, are examples of missing things which do not attract attention but are most apparently absent to anyone looking for such discrepancy. Care must be taken to eliminate only such objects as coincidence would be most unlikely to find unintentionally missing in another person's apparel or equipment.

Cutting an eraser on the end of a pencil into either a wedge shape or a point is a good middle-distance signal. The pencil, point down, would be stuck in the breast pocket of the coat or shirt.

Another middle-distance signal would be the colored thread marking of a handkerchief left protruding from the breast pocket. Such threads are commonly used in many parts of the world by laundries as identification. A colored monogram in a handkerchief can be noticed easily. In either instance, the color used would be the important factor.

Organization lapel buttons, because of their variations in shape, design, and color, are quickly and easily identified. Of course they rarely, if ever, could be used for the purpose under consideration, but the general idea can be followed with pen and pencil clips. The tip of the clip which goes outside the pocket is altered so as to be identifiable. This may be done by filing the clip to change its shape, drilling one or more holes in it, or coloring it with enamel-paint or colored sealing wax. Naturally a specially designed clip is even better, for its distinctive pattern may be so subtle. On another page are suggested designs for altering standard-type clips.

… In such instances where A and B can get within fifteen feet or so of one another, shoelaces make an excellent signaling device. There are several ways in which laces can be used and no one of them ever will be noticed provided the laces are treated identically in both shoes.

The first suggestion is to have the shoelace run as a double strand through the eyelets nearest the instep, i.e., toward the toes. First, the shoestring is cut in half. Then the tip of one lace is pushed from the inside of the shoe up through one hole, across the instep, and down through the opposite hole. The tip of the other half is treated in the same way but is started from the opposite side. While the cut ends still are outside the shoe, each is tied, with a slipknot, around the other lace. The tips of the laces then are drawn so as to have the two knots inside the shoe and each by one of the eyelets. The shoe then is laced in the normal way. For one who is looking for such a possibility, the double lace is easy to distinguish. It will never be seen by one not particularly looking for it. Though it will not be noticed, it is without reason except to mend a broken lace were the shoes to be examined.

Because shoelaces are inserted in shoes in three standard ways, any deviation in these ways becomes useful for signaling. On other pages are illustrations of the standard ways of lacing shoes and several ways in which shoes could be laced but never are. None of these alternate ways will attract attention, yet each is very obvious to one looking for such a signal.

Using one of these shoelacing patterns is an excellent way to identify a person. Because there are several such patterns, added information could be given by the choice of pattern used. "I have information for you." "I'll follow your instruction." "I have brought another person." What need be said is not for this writer to suggest—merely the means to say it.

Alteration of design (such as with the shoelaces) is almost as much of an attention attractor to the person looking for it as is color. Another design variant is using one different button on a shirt or vest. While the buttons so used may be unlike the other visible buttons in several acceptable ways, the use of a button of a different size is probably the best variation and, generally speaking, such a button is easier to obtain. The button should be but a little larger (or smaller) than the other buttons. When on a shirt, and a tie is worn, the tie must be one which does not cover at least two buttons. The difference in size is known by comparison. Were an outsider to notice an odd-size button—which is most unlikely—he would think that the wearer merely did not have a matching button to replace one he had lost.

… The old schoolboy stunt of sticking a thumbtack in the heel of a shoe might also be useful on some occasions. It is something which could be acquired accidentally and to avoid the possibility of an inadvertent thumbtack being in the heel of the wrong person, the tack used for the signal should be stuck in a specified location on the right heel. To find a tack in a particular spot, in the right heel, and on a particular day, and at a certain place and time, of a second person would be asking too much of coincidence.

A method of attracting attention, and done for that obvious purpose, is yelling. "Hi, Pete," or "Aya, Pedro," or any such call is done for the obvious purpose of getting the attention of the one called. If the caller stands three-quarter view to the person whose attention he actually wishes to attract, rather than the imaginary Pete, the yell will serve its purpose and without connecting the two people. Naturally, as soon as the call is made the caller should wave a greeting to the imaginary Pete, and naturally, there have to be several men in that direction, so no one can know of Pete's nonexistence. This means of attracting attention only is possible where there is a crowd, such as at a railway station, but if the crowd were large enough, it could be the only quick way. The name used should be one found in some form in all languages and in a way be something like the "Hey Rube" call circus people use for emergencies.

Acknowledgment of recognition is most important, for otherwise neither person could be certain of the other having noticed his signal. Further, it would be safest were the acknowledgment of recognition also acknowledged. Were this done, each person would be certain of the other's awareness of his presence.

At a distance, the act of rubbing the back of the neck under the collar can be seen easily. It appears to be a most natural act and does not attract attention, yet it is one which almost never is done. Note that it is not scratching the back of the neck but rubbing it with the balls of the fingers and with the fingers straight.

At a short distance the smoking signals, or drinking signals, might well be used for acknowledgment. It might be best to signal a designated number if such signals are used.

Where the contact is between waiter and patron, or clerk and customer, the acknowledgment could be by the patron asking for something unusual but not too odd. Or the waiter-clerk could offer a service or item that would be the signal of acknowledgment. In each instance, the signal would be verbal but would be without special meaning except to the persons listening for it.

The acknowledgment could be touching the special button, clip, shoelace, etc. by the one who has the original signal. Acknowledgment can use a larger variety of natural methods than would be feasible for the original signals. All that is required is that they be simple, quick, and natural.

… No attempt should be made to know and look for all the various signals and codes suggested in these pages. What have been set down are only suggestions. Some may be thought to be unusable as given, some may be adapted and made of use, and some may be of use solely as starting a trend of thought toward usable methods. The point is that whatever is used must be decided upon long before it ever is needed. Every detail then has to be studied, and fully understood, by everyone who ever may be called upon to use the method. Any material which is successful is good. Success will depend upon people, and when one of the elements is a person, there can be no certainty of success unless that person has full knowledge and understanding. No one can be assured he has such knowledge and understanding until he has actually tried out the method to his satisfaction and under calm circumstances. In actual use there are too many distractions to try to recall unmemorized details.

The Penkovsky Papers – The Prikhodko Lecture

Oleg Penkovsky was one of the West's most successful Soviet "defectors in place". A career officer in the GRU, he resented the impediments placed on his career advancement by his father's background as an anti-Bolshevik in the Russian Civil War (1917–22), and in August 1960 made contact with the US Embassy in Moscow, offering to defect. After an initial period of suspicion that his actions might be a provocation, he began passing information to the British. In the 18 months Penkovsky worked for the CIA and MI6, he provided a wealth of vital information which informed Western policymaking, particularly during the Cuban Missile Crisis, when the inside knowledge of Khrushchev's intentions allowed the Americans to outwit the Soviets. Penkovsky finally came under suspicion after being observed handing over material during a "brush contact". The KGB gained access to his apartment, bugged it and gained the evidence needed to convict him of treason.

Penkovsky's fate is unknown – he was probably shot – but his loss, and the cessation of the flow of practical information he had provided on the organization of the KGB and GRU, as well as on Soviet weapons capabilities, proved a bitter blow for US and British intelligence. Among the documents he had smuggled out was a lecture by Lieutenant-Colonel Ivan Prikhodko, of the GRU's Anglo-American Affairs Directorate, which provided a manual for Soviet spies operating in the USA. Prikhodko warns many times of the capabilities of American counter-intelligence, referring to the FBI's placing of tracking devices in automobiles and even the use of X-rays to screen baggage for suspicious devices. As well as practical tips such as the employment of "cut-outs" (trusted intermediaries) to evade surveillance, the use of portable VHF radios and the most efficient design of dead drops (cardboard tubes, old clocks and cigarette packets being suitable receptacles for secret messages), the lecture provides priceless insights into the sometimes inept attempts of the GRU to gain insights into the average American's way of thinking. "It is customary," the prospective agent is told, "to change white shirts and socks daily", and that although golf courses are recommended as a discreet place to brief contacts, the agent is advised that in order to hold meetings there: "An essential requirement is to know the game and how to play."

THE PENKOVSKY PAPERS – THE PRIKHODKO LECTURE

Characteristics of Agent Communications and of Agent Handling in the U.S.A.

Lieutenant-Colonel I. E. Prikhodko

Training Manual

1. Characteristics of Agent Communications

The methods and organisation of agent communication depend basically on the nature of operating conditions.

The way of life, customs, temper, demeanour, and personality traits of Americans have certain well-defined characteristics. The majority of Americans are energetic, enterprising and open people, possessing a great sense of humour. They have considerable business ability and are resourceful, courageous, and industrious.

The absolute power of money in the U.S.A. arouses one desire in many people—to make more money. In describing people Americans often use the expression, "He knows how to make money," which means that that person has a lot of money. The other side of the question, namely, where the money comes from or how it is "made," does not, as a rule, interest anybody. Americans encourage any method of getting rich. American bourgeois propaganda strives in every way to convince the population that everyone can make money if he is resourceful enough. A one-sided upbringing engenders in a part of the population a certain indifference to everything that is not connected with business, profits, and gain. An American's circle of interests is often rather small. Many Americans do not read books. Their main interest lies in advertisements, sport news, and cartoons; on the front pages they only glance at the large sensational headlines.

In general, bourgeois society demoralises people.

Every American family tries to save money for a "rainy day"; therefore, a certain amount is set aside from each pay cheque.

The monopolists do everything possible to keep Americans from devoting their free time to meditative and intellectual activity.

Movies, cheap concerts, boxing, parks, horse races, baseball, football, restaurants—all are used to divert the masses from the realities around them.

An American's wants generally consist of having his own automobile, a comfortable apartment, and a good time. Most Americans, men and women, smoke.

Americans pay much attention to clothes and outward appearances. They try always to have a clean suit, well-pressed with a good crease in the trousers, a clean shirt, and shoes well-polished. They send their suits regularly to the cleaner and their shirts to the laundry, both of which are everywhere in the U.S.A. It is customary to change white shirts and socks daily. Clothing styles in the country change yearly. Just as one can determine accurately from definite features the year of make of an automobile, so can one determine from outward appearances the class level of any American. Despite the fact that style changes frequently, one can still point out several general characteristic features of American dress: narrow and short trousers, short sleeves, white shirt with a starched collar (on official occasions), and always with a necktie. Light colours predominate in clothing. Americans like loose-fitting shoes, as a rule one or two sizes larger than necessary. In his free time, away from work, and especially during the summer, the American dresses in sports clothes: light trousers, short-sleeved shirts, no neck-tie. Sun glasses are widely used. An American's behaviour outside his place of business is free and unconstrained. Many Americans like to keep their hands in their pockets and chew gum.

Agent communications and agent handling involve first and last working with people, as a rule from the bourgeois world. For this work to be successful, it is necessary to know these people well, their characteristics and their personality traits, and the political and economic circumstances which condition their behaviour. An intelligence officer who does not know the characteristics of the American way of life or who neglects those aspects cannot be a fully-fledged agent handler. Thus, for example, a case officer who looks slovenly will not command respect from an agent. If an agent is insufficiently dedicated to our intelligence service, the result of this and similar errors on the part of an intelligence officer may create an impression in the agent's mind that he is dealing with an inadequate and unreliable organisation.

In the organisation and operation of agent communications, knowledge of the local area and local conditions is of the utmost importance. Not only the country as a whole, but even every city, has its own characteristic features which influence agent communications. They may complicate them or, on the contrary, facilitate them.

New York, for example, is distinguished by its large size and its great number of parks, museums, athletic grounds, movie houses, libraries, and other public establishments. A large part of the population consists of people of the most varied nationalities. The city public transport system, especially the subway, is well-developed, and there are a great number of buses and taxis.

In New York it is easy to establish a cover story for going downtown either during the day or at night, since New York has many public places. By making skilful use of transport facilities one can keep a good check on surveillance. Finally, an intelligence officer who speaks with an accent in New York is quite acceptable since many New Yorkers speak with an accent.

There are many large cities in the U.S.A., among which are such giants as New York, Chicago, San Francisco, etc. The large cities in the U.S.A. offer favourable conditions for the organisation of agent communications and for the establishment of a cover story for them.

On the other hand the organisation and operation of agent communications in Washington are fraught with difficulties because of the city's small size, its limited number of public places, the absence of subways, and the poorly developed public transport system, especially in the outskirts.

As we know, there are essentially two types of agent communication: personal and impersonal.

Since they do not involve personal contact between case officer and agent, impersonal communications afford the greatest degree of secrecy and they greatly complicate the work of counter-intelligence in identifying and uncovering our intelligence officers.

In the U.S.A., a country with a highly developed counter-intelligence service, the basic type of agent communication is impersonal communication, the importance of which is continually growing. Operational agents must be able to make good use of impersonal communications and constantly improve them.

However, never forget that proper agent handling and the achievement of the greatest effectiveness in working with agents requires periodic personal meetings with them.

1. Personal Communications

Only by personal contact can the case officer study the agent better, analyse his motives, check on and control his activities, and finally—and this is of great importance—instruct the agent, train him in new methods and in professional intelligence skills, develop him, and exert an influence on him through personal example.

The basic forms of direct communication are the meeting, the recognition meeting and communication through a cut-out or transmission points.

Meetings. A meeting between case officer and agent is one of the most vulnerable forms of communication. Therefore, in organising a meeting, an intelligence officer must anticipate everything in order to guarantee security.

In organising a meeting, the closest attention should be given to such questions as the time, the place and the agenda for the meeting, the cover story for the meeting, and the measures for guaranteeing security.

Meetings should be held at various times of the day, on different days of the week, and on different dates of the month. For example, meetings should not be held on the fifth day of each month, on Wednesday of every week, or consistently at 8.00 p.m., because such uniformity in the activities of an intelligence officer helps the work of counter-intelligence. In fact, in order to compromise an operation it would be enough for counter-intelligence to intensify its surveillance on our case officer for only one day of the month (for example, the fifth of the month), for one day of the week (for example, on Wednesday), and even for only a certain time—until 8.00 p.m.

Neither, however, should there be indiscriminate juggling with times. In selecting a time for a meeting, one should take into consideration the agent's job, his hours of work, his family situation, and the meeting place and area. Maximum consideration should be given to enabling the agent plausibly to explain his absence from work or his departure from home.

Most Americans spend their days off and holidays with their families or with relatives and friends. Besides this, an agent has family holidays—birthdays of family members. An officer must take these factors into consideration, listen to the agent's views, and not arrange a meeting on days which are holidays for the agent and for members of his family.

Most meetings are held in the evening. As a rule, the agent finishes work in the evening and does not have to ask leave of his boss. Besides this, evenings provide the greatest security. However, it is not advisable to hold meetings in a park, because, unlike Europeans, Americans visit parks only during the day. With the approach of darkness nobody uses the parks. At that time of the day only criminal elements and mentally ill persons are to be found in the parks. The press prints special warnings of the danger in going to parks in the evening. Not infrequently the newspapers publish detailed accounts of rapes and murders which were committed in the parks during the night.

It is also possible to hold meetings in the middle of the day and during lunch (Americans have their lunch from 1.00 to 2.00 p.m.). If it falls within his pattern of activities, the agent may absent himself from his office during the day. If this is the case, naturally one can meet him at any time of the day.

Finally, meetings can be held in the morning, before work, since the majority of office workers start work at 9.00 a.m. and some even at 10.00 a.m.

It is known that at certain periods, which may last from one to several months, counter-intelligence concentrates its main efforts on working days during the working hours of Soviet installations, while during pre-holiday days and holidays, as well as during the morning hours, only preventive measures are in force. Our intelligence officers must always consider all aspects of the counter-intelligence agents' *modus operandi* and conduct their clandestine activities during those days and hours when counter-intelligence is least active. The selection of times and dates must always be agreed upon with the agent.

Meetings should, as a rule, be as short as possible; therefore, very careful preparations are necessary. In organising communications from another country, or from the Centre to the U.S.A., and especially in organising radio communications, one should remember the

American practice of changing the time during the summer to be one hour ahead of standard time. Clocks are moved ahead one hour (so-called summer or daylight time, "daylight saving time") starting at 2.00 a.m. on the last Sunday in April and ending at 2.00 a.m. on the last Sunday in September, when clocks are moved back one hour throughout the U.S.A., with the exception of Indiana and Nebraska where daylight time is in effect throughout the year.

In selecting a meeting place, it is of course necessary to take into account the characteristics of the area. Conditions in the city of New York for example, as a whole are favourable for the organisation of agent communications. However, not all areas of the city are suitable for this. For example, of New York's five sections, which are called "boroughs," Richmond is less suitable than the other areas for organising agent communications. This is largely explained by its isolation from the main city. One can get to the island only by ferry (ferry crossings for Richmond are made from Manhattan and from Brooklyn) or by the bridge connecting Richmond with Bayonne and Jersey City. …

…

As a rule, an operation can be compromised through the wrong selection of a meeting place. For example an officer, who was not well acquainted with the city, once selected a meeting place with an agent on a street corner in the evening. There was a large bank on this corner. The case officer appeared for the meeting exactly at the appointed time. The agent was late. The case officer was there for less than two minutes when a policeman approached, asked what he was doing there, and requested him to move on. The case officer had to leave quickly. Moreover, two plain-clothes men followed him until they saw him enter a subway station. The meeting was frustrated.

In another case, the place selected for a recognition meeting was a bus stop served by only one bus line. Our intelligence officer who was supposed to meet an agent at an appointed time arrived at the meeting place. To ensure the security of the meeting, another intelligence officer carried out observation while seated on a bench in a square near the meeting place. Since the agent did not appear for the meeting that day, both intelligence officers went home. This was repeated twice more. On the third day the agent himself approached our intelligence

officer, not the one waiting for him at the bus stop, but the one sitting
on the bench in the square and made contact with him. It transpired
that the agent had passed the meeting place each time, had sat on a
bench in the square and watched the intelligence officers. He decided
not to appear at the bus stop, since he considered it unnatural to wait
there because of the difficulty of having a cover story. It was only on
the third day that the agent became convinced that the man sitting in
the square was a Soviet intelligence officer and approached him, since
he considered the square a more appropriate meeting place.

The most suitable boroughs for meetings are the Bronx, Brooklyn
and Queens, as well as various parts of Manhattan (the area near
Columbia University, the area adjoining Riverside Park, the area east
of Lexington Avenue, and others).

It is essential to select a meeting place that provides security and
convenience for the holding of the meeting. It must also be such that
an appearance there can be explained plausibly and convincingly by
a cover story. Among such places are crowded streets, parks, sports
grounds, sports clubs, restaurants, motels, beaches, etc. ...

    ...

Parks can serve as meeting places. As a rule, New York parks
are grassy fields with only occasional patches of trees and bushes.
There are many sports grounds, etc., in the parks. The footpaths are
asphalt. Main roads often pass through the parks.

The parks in Washington are even more distinctive. They are usually
covered with leafy woods and are cut through by main roads near which
there are a number of parking places and picnic areas. As a rule, there are
no footpaths. It is not customary to take walks through the parks.

There is no charge for entering any of the parks. The populace
makes considerable use of them for resting, sports and exercise. Walking on the grass is permitted in many parks.

Most sports clubs are open to the public, including foreigners. Golf
is the most popular sport of the well-to-do. Agent meetings can be
held at golf courses as easily as in other sports clubs. During the week
(on working days) there are very few people at the golf courses. During these days the officer and his agent can arrive at the golf course
(preferably at different times, twenty to thirty minutes apart), each can
go out to play alone, and at a designated time can meet at, let us say, the

16th hole or at some other hole (there are a total of 18 holes). Saturdays and Sundays are less suitable days for conducting agent activities at golf courses, because on these days many players gather, competitions are held and private play is not permitted. Golf courses are located on the edges of forests or parks in broken terrain where there are many concealed areas. These concealed areas are the most suitable places for holding meetings. In individual cases, meetings can be held in clubhouse restaurants.

In order to hold meetings at golf courses successfully, one must learn the conditions there in advance. An essential requirement is to know the game and how to play. Therefore, students should learn this game while still at the Academy.

Club membership is relatively expensive, and not all clubs are equally accessible to you. It is even difficult for local inhabitants, to say nothing of foreigners, to get into some golf courses, if they do not occupy a certain position in society.

As a rule, a candidate member must be recommended by two or three club members.

New York has golf courses in Pelham Bay Park, Van Courtland Park (the Bronx); in Diker Beach Park (Brooklyn); in Forest Park and Allen Park (Queens); in la Turette Park and Silver Lake Park (Richmond); and others. With club memberships so difficult to obtain it is advisable to use public golf courses.

New York and Washington have numerous restaurants, many of them representing different nationalities. Every restaurant has its own distinctive characteristics. One specialises in steaks (the most expensive steaks are sirloin and T-bone steak), another in seafood; some restaurants have orchestras, others have not. Before selecting a certain restaurant as a meeting place, you must learn everything about that restaurant; the system of service, the type of customers, whether it is in bad repute with the police, etc.

It is the practice in all restaurants to tip the waitress 10 per cent of the amount shown on the check.

Depending on the nature of the agent operation, the officer and agent may sit at the same table and hold the meeting over dinner. Or they may sit at separate tables, maintaining only visual contact for the purpose of exchanging pre-arranged signals, and hold the meeting later on the street after leaving the restaurant. Restaurants are widely used as a refuge from bad, rainy weather.

Americans like to pass the time in bars. Many bars have no tables. Customers occupy high round stools right next to the counter. As a rule, bars do not have snacks or hot dishes. One can only order something to drink: whisky, gin, beer, etc. In order not to attract undue attention the intelligence officer must know how to order well enough; for example, to ask, "Give me a glass of beer." It is also necessary to cite a brand of beer, ("Schlitz," "Rheingold," etc.). In order to keep the customers occupied, most proprietors install a television set in a corner above the bar. Customers often sit over a glass of beer for several hours watching television programmes.

It is most advisable to hold meetings in small restaurants located in the residential area of a city.

The American pharmacy (drug store) does not resemble European pharmacies. Its assortment of goods is not limited to medicines. In many pharmacies one can buy the latest newspaper or magazines, buy food, have a cup of coffee, or make a telephone call. American pharmacies, especially in the large cities, have turned into virtual department stores. Therefore, they are never without customers. Pharmacies can be used to hold short meetings, as well as for other agent activities (signalling, clandestine phone calls).

Along the highways between cities and near cities are many motels. A motel is a small roadside hotel where many people travelling by car can spend the night. It is convenient to hold meetings in a hotel of this type. As a rule, there is always a vacancy. The proprietor always writes down the registration number of the car and the driver's name in a special blank register. No registration is required of other passengers.

Every motel room has a separate entrance. One can leave the motel at any time. Also, the proprietor need not be informed in advance of one's departure. As a rule, people leave a motel early in the morning. The bill is paid at the time the room is rented.

It is advisable to use motels in cases where it is necessary to hold a long meeting with an agent in a closed and isolated location, e.g., when it is necessary to train an agent in radio or in the use of operational techniques. The ability to park the car near one's room or in a nearby garage ensures the covert unloading of equipment.

Even American cinemas have distinctive characteristics. Most cinemas in the large cities are open from 12.00 noon to 1.00 a.m. Film-goers enter as soon as they get their tickets and they may take any unoccupied seat. The filmgoer leaves at any time he wishes, but, as a rule, he leaves when another showing begins. Films are shown without intervals. Americans are not content with a single feature film. Thus, cinema proprietors show two films in succession, which last three to four hours.

Intelligence officers can make wide use of cinemas when organising agent communications by spending some time in them before a meeting. The fact is that there are few people in most cinemas, especially on week days during working hours. Cinemas that are at some distance from the centre of the city are often practically empty. Thus, by arriving at a designated time at a previously determined cinema and taking advantage of the many empty seats, the intelligence officer and agent can hold a meeting inside the cinema. Alternatively, they can use the foyer where there are frequently many vending machines selling cigarettes, cold drinks, chewing gum, etc.

Agent meetings can also be held in outdoor cinemas (drive-in theatres) where films are watched from one's car.

In the U.S.A., where the counter-intelligence effort is highly developed, planning and preparation for a meeting are of the greatest importance. In planning a meeting it is necessary to give maximum consideration to the above-mentioned characteristics of the people and of the country, the working and family situation of the agent, his capabilities, etc. As far as the intelligence officer himself is concerned, he should thoroughly analyse his own conduct. All his activities, his daily routine, his appearances in the city, and his visits to cinemas, libraries and sporting events must be subordinated to one purpose—achieving a more flexible and covert system of agent communications. In this connection all his activities must be natural and plausible.

In planning a meeting, you must consider the place, the kind of place and the time of the previous meeting, in order that the next meeting be held at a different place and, if possible, at a different time.

In New York, for example, it is possible to alternate the use of the different "boroughs"—the Bronx, Queens, Brooklyn and Manhattan.

At the same time that a meeting place is selected, places must be provided along the route to the meeting place where signals can be posted. Signals can be placed along this route to cancel a meeting. This is done with the help of electronic means in those cases when it is established that the officer who is on his way to an agent is under surveillance. Before going to the meeting place, the officer must ascertain that there are no signals which cancel the meeting.

How to leave for a meeting must be thoroughly thought out. It is especially important that those officers working in *rezidentsii* under cover know how to leave their office naturally at a normal and plausible time, how to explain their visits to specific public places and how to make their "check-ups" along the route. The continuity and systematisation of agent communication depend on such knowledge.

Under present-day working conditions, one should set out for meeting not later than two to three hours before the scheduled time. During this time one must check along the stipulated route to detect any surveillance by the counter-intelligence service. If surveillance is detected, carry out the cover reason for leaving then return to the point of departure to make another attempt at· leaving. At times the intelligence officer will have to make several tries before he succeeds in evading surveillance. In most cases, therefore, the intelligence officer leaves his office quite early. If, for example, on the day of a meeting, while on his way to or from lunch, an intelligence officer notices that he is not being watched, there is no need for him to go home for lunch or to return to work after lunch. He goes to the city, conducts another very careful check, spends the rest of his time in a cinema or some other place which affords security, and appears at the meeting place at the appointed time.

Several examples are given below which illustrate an intelligence officer's method of leaving for a meeting and the nature of his actions.

An intelligence officer had a Sunday meeting scheduled for the latter part of the day. After breakfast he took his family for a walk in the park. He usually took such a walk every Sunday. On the way he invited a friend. The two families selected some benches in the park and seated themselves in the sun. The adults conversed and looked through newspapers and magazines which they had bought at a stand, while the children played nearby. They all went to the zoo together, and they also looked at some monuments. While passing a cinema, they noticed the advertising display and decided to see the new film. They all went inside. The intelligence officer who had a meeting scheduled quickly departed through a side door and left for the meeting place along a previously selected route. The meeting was held successfully. Towards evening the intelligence officer and his family returned home after a restful Sunday.

In another case, a meeting was scheduled for a Monday evening. After work on Saturday, the intelligence officer left for the country cottage where some families spent all summer and where most of the Soviet officials spent Saturdays and Sundays. Monday morning, as usual, he returned to the city in his car. On the way, observing that he was not under surveillance he decided to take advantage of this opportunity. He did not go to work but parked his car instead on a street (some distance from his place of business—and from the meeting place). He then boarded a subway and went to a different part of the city. He got off the subway at a little-used station and confirmed the absence of surveillance; he then bought a newspaper and again boarded the subway. Later the intelligence officer got off at another station and went to an automat restaurant for breakfast. Again there was no surveillance. After breakfast the intelligence officer made several more trips on the subway and fully confirmed the absence of surveillance. To avoid being detected on the streets by the counter-intelligence service, the intelligence officer went into a cinema. Twenty to thirty minutes before the scheduled meeting, he left the movie theatre and went to the meeting place, again checking along the way. The meeting took place at the appointed time.

The intelligence officer must think through in advance all such problems connected with the planning and conduct of a meeting, including possible variations of departures and make a report for the *rezident*.

Conducting a meeting is the principal phase of agent operation. Meetings play an essential role in the training of an agent. Therefore, they should be conducted in a precise, planned, and specific manner, with a thorough knowledge of the case and with attention given to all circumstances. During the meeting the officer must not only stipulate the order of the meeting with the agent and the cover story for the meeting, review the conditions for the alternate meeting, listen to the agent's report, and assign him tasks, but he must also instruct him in various matters, listen to his questions and give him competent answers. The officer must take a constant interest in the agent's personal affairs and environment so that the agent can be cautioned in advance, if need be, about possible errors in his conduct.

Since meetings should not be too lengthy the intelligence officer must be well prepared for each meeting. During the meeting he must be alert to catch the most fleeting changes in the agent's mood. To a large extent, an officer's authority depends on his conduct, his discussion of operational matters, the ability to conceal the fatigue which he might be feeling after a long trip and many security checks. Nor should he show any nervousness, no matter what the external reasons might be. If the officer exhibits stability and self-control, the agent will acquire confidence in working with our intelligence service.

Despite the fact that very important problems are being considered at a meeting, it is most desirable that the case officer should have a sense of humour, which is valued highly by American agents, be able to tell jokes appropriately, and enliven the conversation. This helps to establish good rapport with the agent.

Recommendations on the Conduct of Intelligence Officers Engaged in Personal Communications. The conduct of an intelligence officer has a direct bearing on his work with agents. The people with whom the intelligence officer comes in contact must be convinced that all his actions and his conduct are determined by his job, by the nature of his personal life and by his cultural tastes. It is necessary to accustom those around him to a pattern of activities which readily includes agent work. To overcome the hindrances of counter-intelligence, our intelligence officers, besides following the general rules of intelligence operations, must adopt special measures and actions. The intelligence officers in *rezidentsii* under cover, who are under constant surveillance by the counter-intelligence service, are particularly compelled to make considerable use of these measures.

It is known that counter-intelligence static observation posts carefully record the time that all employees of Soviet installations arrive for work and the time they depart. The counter-intelligence service can draw up charts on the arrival and departure of our colleagues and use them to organise their surveillance. In order to invalidate such "charts" and not give the counter intelligence service the opportunity to establish any kind of regular or recurrent pattern of the length of time our colleagues stay inside a building, trips to the city on operational matters must be covered by disguising them. Such trips are carried out under the guise of conducting personal activities—visits to cinemas, museums, exhibitions, and athletic events, shopping, etc.

While making a trip to the city, the intelligence officer checks for surveillance. Once he is convinced that he is not under surveillance, the intelligence officer uses this trip into town to improve his knowledge of it, to select new meeting places, dead-drops and places for posting signals, and to select and confirm routes along which a check can be made for surveillance. If he detects surveillance, the intelligence officer must act according to a previously conceived cover plan: he can act like a person who has a great interest in books and, consequently, visit a number of book stores, or he can pretend to be a baseball enthusiast, the most popular sport in the U.S.A. It would not be a bad idea if an intelligence officer could create the impression that he is fond of taking walks about the city. At the same time, he must learn the methods of surveillance. Under no circumstances must he show that he has detected the surveillance, in order not to reveal his familiarity with the *modus operandi* of the counter-intelligence service. Likewise, an intelligence officer who is under surveillance should not exhibit nervousness or do anything which is unnatural.

It is advisable to analyse each trip into town, to draw conclusions on the operating methods of the counter-intelligence service and on the city and public places. These conclusions should be written down in a special notebook. Gradually the intelligence officer will acquire a collection of very valuable material.

American stores periodically hold sales of their merchandise at lowered prices. During the first days of the sale a large number of people usually gather at the store. In their efforts to advertise the sale of merchandise, the proprietors invite newspaper photographers to the opening of the sale. To avoid being caught by the reporter's lens, our intelligence officers and members of their families should not visit the store during the first days of the sale.

It is recommended that intelligence officers take frequent walks about the city at various times. Depending on his work load and the purpose for the walks, he can do so in the evening after work, in the morning before work and during his lunch hour. After he "accustoms" the counter-intelligence service to such walks, the intelligence officer can use them later to support agent communications (posting or checking of signals), agent meetings, servicing dead-drops, etc.

Every intelligence officer who handles agents must have previously selected and well-studied counter-surveillance check routes which afford the most favourable opportunities for the detection of surveillance.

A counter-surveillance check route may include travel by automobile (which is then parked on a side street or some city garage); the use of sparsely populated streets, especially in those areas where parallel surveillance is precluded; travel by subway with several transfers at empty stations; visits to large stores and other buildings with numerous lifts, entrances and exits, and which also have direct access to subways (Pennsylvania Station, Macy and Saks department stores, Chrysler Building, and others).

At the same time that such routes are being selected, a good cover story should also be developed to explain the intelligence officer's presence in this or that area.

If he detects surveillance, the intelligence officer must not go to meet the agent; but he must spend some time naturally in the city, convince the counter-intelligence agents of the need for his being in the city, and then return home. The surveillance agents will thus have to report that their man was not detected committing any inappropriate act.

Generally, as we mentioned, there is no particular need for the intelligence officer to return to the *rezidentsia* late after an evening meeting. It is advisable therefore, to inform the *rezident* about the meeting by passing or posting a predetermined signal: "Meeting held; all is well," or "Meeting did not take place," etc. The nature of the signal will depend on specific conditions: the working and personal relationships between the officer and *rezident*, etc. The signal can be taken by the *rezident* himself, by his chauffeur, or by any other intelligence operative who is not busy that day. A detailed report on the operation can be made the following day.

The counter-intelligence service of the U.S.A. considers all Soviet employees as potential intelligence officers and constantly strives to determine which of them has special work to do. With this goal in mind, a number of measures are employed, the main ones of which are eavesdropping (in apartments, in automobiles, on the street, etc.), surveillance, and the study and analysis of the conduct of Soviet employees. With this fact in mind, the intelligence officer must not discuss operational matters outside the confines of the specially equipped room in the *rezidentsia* and he must conduct himself so as not to arouse the suspicion of those around him. It is very important that he avoid establishing a pattern in intelligence work.

In organising agent communications the intelligence officer will frequently have to make use of the city transport system. The *subway* occupies first place in New York in the volume of passenger traffic and therefore is the basic mode of transport.

There are no ticket collectors on the subway. Special metal revolving gates are situated at the entrance. The ticket office does not sell tickets but metal tokens which cost fifteen cents. On passing through the revolving gate, the passenger inserts the token in a special slot. An intelligence officer should always have several tokens with him, especially on the day of a meeting, so that he does not waste any time in buying them at the entrance to the subway.

It is difficult to imagine how an operation for maintaining agent communications can be conducted in New York without using the subway which, despite its complexity, is an excellent means of getting about. It also affords a convenient place to check on the existence or absence of surveillance.

A poor knowledge of the city's means of transport, especially the subway, can sometimes lead to the disruption of an agent meeting. The following example will underline this point:

Our officer left for a meeting at the appropriate time. After carrying out a carefully planned check, he was convinced that he was not under surveillance. Twenty minutes remained until the meeting. During that time he had to go to the meeting place and once more confirm the absence of surveillance. According to his plan, he was to use the subway for this purpose. At a certain station he boarded a subway going in the opposite direction from the meeting place, and planned to get off at the next station and then double back to the meeting place.

There were practically no passengers in the subway car. A man took a seat near him, opened a paper and engrossed himself in reading.

The officer passed one stop and then got off. The man with the newspaper, as though suddenly recollecting something, quickly folded his newspaper and also got off the subway. The intelligence officer became wary. He boarded the next train and sat down. The man with the newspaper took a seat in the same car and again became absorbed in his paper. The intelligence officer became rattled—this was obvious surveillance. He rode past his stop. The man with the newspaper did not seem to be paying any attention to him. Finally, the intelligence officer could endure it no longer and got off the subway. The unknown man did not even lift his head and rode on. None of the passengers got off. The intelligence officer went out on the street and conducted a check—no external surveillance. But it was already too late to make the meeting. He made another check, confirmed the absence of surveillance then went home. An important meeting was disrupted.

It later transpired that the intelligence officer at first had taken a local train, had passed his stop, and had then taken an express going in the opposite direction. Local residents often do the same thing, when they have a long way to go. They get on at the nearest intermediate station and take a train going in the direction of the nearest express stop and then transfer to an express. Our officer did not take this into consideration, because he did not know subway conditions well.

Buses stop at the request of passengers. Before the stop at which he wants to get off, the passenger must pull a special cord overhead which serves as a signal to the driver. In addition, the driver stops the bus when signalled by passengers waiting at a stop, providing, however, that there is room on the bus.

Buses operate without conductors.

One enters a bus through the front door and leaves through the rear door. Near the driver is a small meter in the form of a small box into which the passenger deposits fifteen cents in New York and twenty cents in Washington. The bus driver controls the entrance and departure of passengers, gives change, and gives out transfers (at the request of the passenger). He changes banknotes, but only up to five dollars. Therefore, the intelligence officer must always be certain that he has change or one-dollar bills.

Tickets are not used on buses. The method of using streetcars is the same as the one for buses.

Taxis do not have stands. Moreover, they are not permitted to stop on the street for any length of time, because the traffic is so dense. Taxis are always on the move and only stop for passengers. A taxi can be stopped anywhere; this is done merely by signalling with the hand or by loudly shouting, "Taxi," when an empty one passes.

The taxi driver enters in a log the place a fare entered the taxi, the place he got out, and the time. Therefore, an intelligence officer must never take a taxi directly to the meeting place. To make proper use of taxis in operational work, it is necessary to know a number of addresses in different areas and to be prepared to give a taxi driver a destination at a moment's notice.

In the U.S.A., our intelligence officers make wide use of *private cars* (particularly in Washington) not as a place for meeting or talking with an agent, but only as a means of going to the area of the meeting, and of detecting and losing surveillance. The reason is that the counter-intelligence service can secretly install in the cars of Soviet employees special devices which emit a signal giving the vehicle's location.

Cars are very widely used for transport in the U.S.A. The car is an integral part of the way of life of the American family. All the streets in the large cities are packed with cars. To find a free place to park is far from easy. There are not enough garages and parking lots to meet the demand. Nevertheless, there is always room on parking lots and in garages (old multi-story buildings are often converted into garages). This is because their fees are so high. For example, the cost of parking a car in the centre of Manhattan can be as much as seventy-five cents, and even one dollar, for the first hour, up to a maximum of three dollars for the day.

The intelligence officer using an automobile in organising communications must always park his car in a garage or a particular place a considerable distance from the meeting place, or even in a different borough. He should continue his mission using public transport.

There are quite a few companies in the U.S.A. which rent cars on a temporary basis. All that is needed to rent a car is to present one's driving licence and leave a small deposit. It is advisable to use rented cars in the organisation of agent communications, because this affords a number of advantages. For example, an intelligence officer can drive to the city in his own car and, after checking for surveillance, leave it in a suitable area or in a parking lot; he can then go on to complete his task in a rented car. Such use of cars makes the work of the counter-intelligence service more difficult.

The largest car-hire company is the "Hertz-Rent-a-Car-System."

There are a large number of toll bridges and tunnels in the U.S.A. The toll is collected by a policeman on duty (about twenty to twenty-five cents for a one-way trip). It should be assumed that at these points notice is taken of cars with diplomatic plates, especially of those cars whose drivers are employees of Soviet installations. Therefore such places are to be avoided when carrying out intelligence tasks and instead bridges without tolls should be used where it is more difficult to keep track of cars.

[Ed. Note: At this point a page is missing from the original document. ...]

...which can be with initials, with some kind of figure in the form of a stamp or mark, or some kind of special stone. Besides rings, women wear many ornaments around the neck, on the hands, and on their clothing. Depending on the sex of the agent, any of these can be used as a recognition sign.

Americans make widespread use of various wrapping papers with advertisements in the form of writing, photographs, coloured pictures, etc. Small objects (a box of vitamin pills or chewing gum) with a distinctive packaging can also be used as recognition signs.

The most suitable parole is the question, and the countersign, the answer to the question. Both parole and the countersign contain special stipulated words or phrases. The stipulated words can be the names of museums, cinemas, libraries, and monuments or the titles of movies, books, newspapers, magazines, etc. It is essential that both the question and answer be short and simple in content and in pronunciation, because it is difficult to pronounce some English words, especially for intelligence officers who may have just arrived in the country.

In working out the conditions for a recognition meeting and, above all, for the recognition signs, parole and countersign, the intelligence officer has ample opportunity to exhibit his initiative, resourcefulness, and creativity, and to resolve his problems with originality and with the maximum consideration of local conditions.

Communication through Cut-outs and Live Drops. In certain cases it becomes necessary to resort to cut-outs and live drops as a means of effecting communication.

The case officer very carefully trains a cut-out in every separate agent operation: he instructs him, cultivates in him the desired qualities and checks on his efficiency. Even when communication is being carried out through a cut-out, it is still advisable for the case officer periodically to meet the agent to check personally whether the work is proceeding properly and whether the tasks are being properly conveyed to the agent: the officer must take an interest in the relations between the cut-out and the agent in order to exert effective and timely influence over the entire course of the work.

If the agent is in another town, the cut-out must obviously have the opportunity of visiting that town. The following have this opportunity: service personnel of the various types of passenger and freight transport; representatives and agents of trading and manufacturing firms, insurance companies, and real estate offices; correspondents, etc.

The cut-out receives (from the agents) only that information which is needed for his work. As a rule, the addresses and surnames of the case officer and agent are not given to the cut-out.

When communicating by means of a live drop there is no personal contact between the agent operatives. Operational materials from the agent to the case officer, and vice versa, are passed through a special person who more frequently than not is the proprietor of a small private business (book shops, antique dealers, chemists' shops, etc.).

The case officer visits the live drop to receive materials only after a special signal. The proprietor of the live drop places the signal after receiving the material from the agent.

2. Impersonal Communications

Under the complex operating conditions which exist in the U.S.A., the basic type of agent communication is impersonal. Practice has shown that this is the most secure type of communication, because there is no direct contact between agent operatives.

Impersonal communication is used to pass operational materials, to assign tasks, and to pass material and technical supplies to *rezidentsii* and individual agents.

It is effected between the Centre and *rezidentsii,* as well as within residencies.

The basic forms of impersonal communication are radio, dead-drops, postal and telegraph systems, telephone, press, and communications with the aid of signals.

Radio Communications with Rezidentsii. Ultra short wave (V.H.F.) radio sets are used for communications within a *rezidentsia.* These sets greatly increase the efficiency of agent communications. They have a small operating radius. Nevertheless, while it is being used, accidental or organised radio monitoring is possible and our intelligence service must always take this into consideration. The use of specially worked out codes, ciphers, procedure and operating schedules make the use of this set completely secure. Radio signals can be used to summon the agent for an emergency meeting, to inform him when a dead-drop has been loaded or unloaded, to notify him about a change in dead-drops, etc. V.H.F. radio communication can also be used within *rezidentsii* to assign tasks to an agent and to receive intelligence information from an agent. Radio communications over V.H.F. must be brief.

There are many different ways of using a portable V.H.F. set. The following are only some of the uses:

…when the intelligence officer and the agent are moving along different streets;

…when the intelligence officer and the agent are in cars in different parts of the city;

…when the intelligence officer is in town and is transmitting on the move and the agent is receiving at his home;

…when the intelligence officer is on shore, and the agent is in a boat.

To conduct communications via V.H.F., there must be a schedule for radio communications. This schedule provides for a place for each radio station, the exact time for the start of radio communication (date, hour, and minute), which radio station will begin transmitting first, and other questions.

"Dead-Drop" Communication. Dead-drops are widely used for communication within *rezidentsii,* as well as for communications between the Centre and Illegal *rezidentsii,* agent nets, or individual agents.

The use of dead-drops in organising communications with agents has a number of advantages over personal meetings. Some of the principal advantages are:

...dead-drop communications are more secure because there is no direct contact between the officer and agent;

...they are more clandestine, because it is possible for the agent not to know the intelligence officer with whom he is in contact via the dead-drop;

...by using a dead-drop the intelligence officer need not have a good knowledge of the local language;

...in case of need, one intelligence officer can be replaced by another;

...there is wide adaptability in time.

However, the use of dead-drops is not without its drawbacks. The dead-drop is an intermediate link between the officer and agent, and materials placed in a dead-drop are outside the control of agent operatives for a certain period. The length of time during which materials are located in a dead-drop should therefore be kept to a minimum.

In practice, stationary, portable and mobile dead-drops are used.

Stationary dead-drops are selected or specially prepared in parks and squares, in trees, in the ground, in fences, in benches, in monuments, in public buildings and in the country, in such places as forests, fields, seashores, river banks, etc.

In selecting and preparing a dead-drop in a park, it is necessary to bear in mind that a number of American parks (for example, Central Park in New York) have many squirrels which can destroy the dead-drop (especially in hollow trees) and carry off the material.

As a rule, a dead-drop is used only once, after which a new one is used. In agent operations in the U.S.A., it is advisable to adopt a system which can consist of a series of dead-drops for the agent and a certain number for the case officer. It is necessary to work out a schedule for using dead-drops so that the agent will know the numbers for the dead-drops to be used in January, those to be used in February, etc. The schedule can be prepared for a half year or for a full year, depending on the quantity selected.

The use of portable dead-drops is more worthy of consideration, since it is considerably easier to find places for them.

There is no particular difficulty in finding places in American cities which contain many discarded objects (boxes, tubes, bottles, cans, old clocks, cigarette packets, paper, etc.). Frequently, those objects lie in plain sight for long periods of time without arousing any interest or desire to pick them up. Among such objects, which are of no use to anybody, and which can be found in yards, in parks, etc., an agent operative can leave a similar object with agent material concealed in it at a predetermined place to have it picked up later by another agent operative.

In the U.S.A., household articles, medicines, and other merchandise are put out in packages of all types; boxes, cans, tubes, cases, and made of cardboard, metal and plastic. Hence there is an extremely wide selection of packages which can be used as portable dead-drops.

Among the items which can be used as portable dead-drops and which are worked over in advance are pieces of wood, stone, brick, clay, cement, plastic, gypsum and others.

Widespread use can be made of magnetic containers in New York, which has many metallic structures. They can be attached to metal fences, metal poles, etc.

In communication through a dead-drop the agent receives instructions in written form. The contents of these orders must be encoded or enciphered. Besides this, the material itself must be in a form suitable for passing through a dead-drop. Therefore, it is necessary to train the agent in the use of ciphers, codes, the preparation of soft emulsion film, microdot, and secret writing.

The technical knowledge of the average American is fairly high. In his everyday life he makes wide use of machines, apparatus and instruments, which makes the training of an American agent in operational technology all the easier.

The type of signals and the places for posting them in connection with dead-drop communications are the same as those which were discussed in the section, "Characteristics of Other Types of Meetings." It is necessary only to stress the particular importance and convenience of radio means in exchanging signals.

The intelligence officer in the U.S.A. who possesses initiative and imagination will always have unlimited opportunities to use dead-drops in all its aspects when organising agent communications.

One to two days prior to an operation for the loading or unloading of a dead-drop, the agent operative reports his plan for the operation to the *rezident* and receives his orders from him.

Several hours before the time of the operation (not later than $1^{1}/_{2}$ to 2 hours) on the day it is to take place, the agent operative goes to the city. He uses the available time in a thorough check to determine whether he is under surveillance. At the same time he checks a pre-arranged place for a danger signal if such a signal has been provided for. As a rule, the check is carried out away from the area where the dead-drop is located.

Convinced that he is not under surveillance and that there is no danger signal, the agent operative goes to the dead-drop. In the immediate vicinity of the dead-drop he should once more confirm that conditions are favourable; then, without any loss of time, go to the dead-drop, load (unload) it, and proceed on the prescribed course.

On his return trip the agent operative can place his signal that the dead-drop has been loaded (unloaded).

The Clandestine Use of the Postal and Telegraph System. The postal and telegraph systems in the U.S.A. are highly developed. The number of postal operations in the country exceeds several tens of millions. Such a large quantity of correspondence precludes scrutiny of their contents.

This enormous stream of mail sent abroad, as well as inside the country, can be successfully used for intelligence purposes both in peacetime and in war.

The postal and telegraph services work quite efficiently and letters are rarely lost. Thus, we have favourable conditions for using the postal and telegraph systems in agent communication.

The postal and telegraph system is used to send hidden or concealed intelligence information. Intelligence messages must in no
way differ from an ordinary letter of the country, either in superficial
appearance or in their overt contents. ...

In order to have effective agent communications by post or telegraph in wartime, too, the agent must be trained in peacetime in the
use of ciphers, codes, secret writing, and microphotography, and be
provided with accommodation addresses. Another reason why this is
important is that there will be a tightening of postal censorship in
time of war.

There are various methods of organising communications within a *rezidentsia*. The *rezident* can receive correspondence from the
agent either at his home address or at an accommodation address.
Correspondence to the agent can be sent to his home address, to a hotel address, or to a post office box rented by the agent at the post office.

Clandestine Use of the Telephone. The telephone has penetrated deeply into the American way of life. Many business transactions are
conducted by telephone. There are more than four million telephones in New York alone. Besides private and office telephones,
there are also a large number of public telephones. A characteristic
of American public telephones is that they have their own numbers and can receive calls. This can be used when organising agent
communications. At a pre-determined time the intelligence officer
can, for example, talk from a public telephone with an agent who
at a pre-arranged time goes to another previously specified public
telephone. It is advisable to select a telephone in a sparsely populated
area and to use it during working hours when public telephones are
used less frequently. Besides this, public telephones can also be used
as a means of signalling.

The most convenient telephones for an intelligence officer to use
are those in large department stores, subway stations and drugstores.

One can also call any other city from a public telephone. To do this
one calls the operator by putting in ten cents and then states the city
and telephone number of the person being called. In this case, one must
pay an additional sum which the operator will indicate; therefore, the
intelligence officer should have between $1 and $ 1.50 in small change.

Under favourable circumstances the agent's home or office telephone may be used. In both instances the time and the days when the agent is at home and at work must be known to the persons who might answer the phone, also the subjects the agent usually discusses at that time, i.e., they must know all circumstantial details.

The counter-intelligence service in the U.S.A. makes widespread use of telephone tapping; therefore, our intelligence officers who are under cover use the telephone quite rarely and do so clandestinely.

Telephone conversations must be short and well thought out. Special phrases (to designate an emergency meeting or something else) must be strictly within the context of the conversation. Experience shows that individual agents not infrequently forget the communications arrangements, resulting in a break of the work routine. It is, therefore, advisable to check periodically the agent's knowledge of various parts of the communications arrangements, including code words and their meaning.

The following case can serve as an example. A code phrase had been provided for to summon an agent to a meeting from another city. When the need arose, the case officer called the agent at work from a public telephone. The case officer identified himself by his code name and then gave the code phrase, "My wife and I would like to thank you very much for the gift you sent us for our family holiday."

Bewildered, the agent replied, "Who? I? Sent a gift? What gift?" The case officer realised that the agent had forgotten the communications arrangements. He then calmly repeated his name (code name), and then asked, "You apparently didn't recognise me?" He then repeated the code phrase. This time the agent understood what it was all about. He shouted merrily into the receiver, "Sorry; old boy, I didn't recognise you at first. I'm very glad that you both liked my little present." A week later the agent appeared for the emergency meeting.

It is a custom in the U.S.A. to state difficult words, especially surnames, in letter form, i.e., to spell them. (In the U.S.A., the word is first spelled and then, as in England, pronounced.) Our intelligence officer, especially the Illegal intelligence officer, must be able to spell out loud; he must be able to spell any word quickly and unhesitatingly. This is achieved through training. One must prepare very carefully for a telephone conversation to make certain that neither the contents of the conversation nor the speaker's accent would arouse the suspicions of an outsider.

If the use of a telephone is contemplated when organising agent communications, serious consideration should be given to the use of a *cut-out telephone*.

As a rule, a cut-out telephone is called from a public telephone. The conversation is in code and should correspond to the nature of the cut-out telephone owner's work so that it will not vary in the least from the owner's daily telephone conversations. Signals can be given over the telephone (by voice or by rings). In transmitting signals over the telephone, careful attention should be paid to the time set for the signal to be given; times of day, phrases and the number of rings should be changed frequently.

The Use of the Press as a Signalling System. In the U.S.A., there are up to two thousand daily newspapers published with a circulation of about 57 million, and more than seven thousand magazines. Both newspapers and magazines devote considerable space to advertisements and classified announcements. Newspaper companies receive sizeable profits from advertisements and therefore accept them quite readily.

In 1958, for example, readers paid a total of one to one and a half billion dollars in the purchase of newspapers, while financial and industrial chiefs paid the newspaper owners more than three billion dollars for advertising. Thus, the publishing houses receive several times more in profits from advertisements and announcements than they do from the sale of newspapers.

Classified advertisements in American newspapers are extremely varied in content and in length. The most widespread ones concern the sale and rental of housing, the sale of personal effects, jobs, announcements of weddings, divorces, births and deaths, the loss of valuables and pets, etc. Given below are samples of several announcements which can be used in intelligence work.

Position wanted
Housework—Mature Colombian maid speaking a little Eng. will give considerable care to children or invalid lady; do efficient general housework. $25-$30 per wk. Exeter 4-0482, 7-10 p.m.

Domestic Employment
Chauffeur, white—wanted. Age 35 married. Twelve years exp. Intelligent alert neat. Fordham 4-7457 before noon. ...

Lost and Found
Brief case left in taxi Wednesday afternoon Jan. 4th travelling Idlewild Airport to 1506 Woodside Avenue, New York. Reward Dunhill 4-0892, ext. 534.

Cats, Dogs and Birds
Poodle tiny white. Lost in Queens, New Year's Day. Answers to the name "Tiny." $250 reward. Humboldt 6-9016.

As can be seen from these examples, many announcements can quite easily be adapted to the passing of information. Among the code words which can be used are: the names or description of the lost article; a description of the circumstances; the place and time it was lost; the size of the reward for returning the valuable or pet, and so on.

Illegal *rezidentsii* will have the greater opportunity to make use of the Press in the organisation of agent communications. *Rezidentsii* under cover may use the Press on a lesser scale, principally to transmit information or signals from agent to case officer. On the whole, conditions in the U.S.A. are favourable for the use of the Press in intelligence work.

To initiate and maintain impersonal communications, a sum of money is paid to place an advertisement or some kind of announcement in the Press. The text of these advertisements or announcements will contain a prearranged coded secret message.

When organising communications involving the use of the Press, one must specify the particular newspaper or magazine in which the coded intelligence information will appear, the approximate dates of publication, and the form of the correspondence (advertisement, classified announcement, etc.).

The placing of coded announcements in the Press can serve not only as a means of communications within a *rezidensia*, but also with the Centre. In communicating with the Centre the major newspapers which are sent abroad should be used (*New York Times*,

New York Herald Tribune, and others). For communications within a *rezidensia*, however, it is advisable to use small local newspapers, since there is less likelihood of censorship over them and since it is simpler to place announcements in them.

Signalling, as a rule, plays an auxiliary role in communications. When using dead-drops and when holding personal meetings and recognition meetings, intelligence officers use signalling a great deal.

The signals should be varied as much as possible. They must also be natural and must not strike the eye of an outsider by their oddity. They must be sufficiently legible and precise to preclude any misinterpretation.

Agent operatives must exchange signals at a distance while in sight of each other. Various objects may be used for this (handkerchief, gloves, cigarettes), as well as a certain colour of clothing and other methods.

Signals can also be given by specially constructed technical means. To transmit infra-red signals not visible to the eye, a pocket flashlight can be used equipped with a special infra-red light filter. Infrared signals are received with "BI-8" binoculars, which have a special "phosphorous" element for this purpose that changes invisible infrared rays into visible rays.

Signals may be transmitted by placing an announcement in the local press or by sending a postcard, letter or telegram.

Finally, sound signals can be sent by radio or telephone.

Thus, signals can be subdivided into graphic, object, light, sound and personal signals.

Graphic signals are prearranged marks in the form of geometric figures, lines, letters, ciphers, etc., written in pencil or chalk, with a nail or some other sharp object in a previously specified place.

Object signals are various small objects put in a previously specified place. The object itself can serve as a signal; so can its position; or the object and its position together can be a signal.

A thorough study of the country enables one to select the most natural signals. One of our intelligence officers, for example, summoned an agent for an introductory meeting by sending the newspaper *Washington Daily News* to his apartment. The intelligence officer went to the city, conducted a careful check, and then from a public telephone called the newspaper office and requested them to start delivery on the next day to the address he gave them (the agent's address). A week after delivery started, the agent appeared at the previously indicated meeting-place. Signals may also be made by sending the agent books, magazines, or merchandise from self-service stores where the practice of delivering to the home is widespread.

A large variety of signals permits a broad diversification in the use of signals and prevents patterns of activity. Certain signals (graphic and object) are used in connection with dead-drops; others (light signals, and sound signals transmitted by phone or radio) are used to call for a meeting and to warn of danger; the third group (signals given by radio and signals given through the use of the mails or Press) is used for communicating with the Centre or with an agent living in another city.

Therefore the selection of signals and the methods for sending them depend on the circumstances, the tasks to be carried out, and the situation of the agent operatives.

CHAPTER 2

ORGANIZATION

Soviet Military Intelligence – Suvorov on the Undercover Residency

The intelligence services of the various competing powers during the Cold War formed complex, often overlapping networks. The GRU, Soviet Military Intelligence, operated alongside, but independently of the KGB from its foundation in 1918, but always concentrated on external threats to the USSR, rather than internal subversion. Vladimir Rezun was a major in the GRU who was serving as an assistant military attaché in Vienna when he defected to the British in 1978. Using the cover name Viktor Suvorov, he subsequently wrote several books about Soviet military intelligence, providing illuminating details about the ways in which GRU *Rezidentura* ("residencies") operated abroad.

The undercover Resident was not acknowledged as an intelligence operative to the officials of his host country, and the GRU Resident ran operations, recruited agents and communicated with Moscow quite separately from his KGB Resident colleague. The smallest residencies only had a cipher officer to encrypt telegrams back to the Centre in the USSR, but more important posts had a deputy resident, Operational Office (in charge of agent recruitment), Technical Services Officer (for bugging and radio monitoring) and Operation Technical Officers (who organized dead-letter drops, agent security and counter-surveillance protocols). The GRU's tentacles, as Rezun explains, did not end at the embassy, with the local branches of Aeroflot, the Soviet airline, being under its supervision (just as the KGB controlled Intourist, the Soviet state travel agency).

The various types of agents controlled by the *Rezidentura* varied: "Head Agents" were the leader of an entire network; "Executive agents" carried out direct operations such as assassinations or sabotage; "Legalisers" worked to validate the cover stories of illegals by providing them with passports and other documentation; "Couriers" carried messages back and forth from Moscow; and "Sources", the backbone of the operation, provided the GRU (or KGB) with secret information. Although some, such as Kim Philby and Guy Burgess, operated in the upper echelons of the intelligence services whose secrets they were betraying to the Soviet Union, this was not necessarily the case. As Rezun remarked, "It is clearly unnecessary to recruit an officer from the Ministry of Defence, if one can recruit his secretary."

SOVIET MILITARY INTELLIGENCE – SUVOROV ON THE UNDERCOVER RESIDENCY

Chapter Two

The Undercover Residency

The undercover residency is one of the basic forms of intelligence set-up for the GRU abroad. (It should be remembered that the undercover residency and the illegal residency are completely separate entities.) In every country where official Soviet representation exists there is a GRU undercover residency. It exists in parallel with, and is analogous to, the KGB undercover residency. Thus every overseas Soviet colony is invisibly divided into three organisations: the 'clean ones', that is the genuine diplomats and correspondents, and the representatives of external trade, civil airlines, the merchant navy, and Intourist, headed by the ambassador; the undercover residency of the GRU; and the undercover residency of the KGB.

Very often, the 'clean' personnel make no distinction between the KGB and the GRU and call them both dirty, 'savages', 'Vikings' or 'neighbours'. The more enlightened staff, like for example the ambassador, his senior diplomats and the more observant people, understand the difference between the two organisations, dividing them up as close neighbours (the KGB), who continually meddle in the day-to-day affairs of each person in the colony, and distant neighbours who take absolutely no interest at all in the day-to-day life of the Soviet colony (the GRU).

For the GRU undercover residency lives a secluded and isolated life. It contains significantly fewer employees than either of the other organisations. Normally in Soviet colonies up to 40 per cent of the people may be considered in the 'clean' category. (This of course does not prevent the majority of them, to a greater or lesser extent, from co-operation with both the KGB and the GRU; but they are not to be considered as professional intelligence officers.) Up to 40 or 45 per cent are officers of the KGB and only 15 to 20 per cent, in rare cases up to 25 per cent, are officers of the GRU. This does not however mean that the intelligence potential of the GRU apparatus is less than that of the KGB. The larger part of the KGB personnel is occupied with questions of security, that is with the collection of compromising material on Soviet people, 'clean' people including the ambassador, and their own colleagues in the KGB who have contact with foreigners and frequently with officers of the GRU. Only a small proportion, in optimum cases half of the KGB personnel, are working against foreigners. The GRU, on the other hand, directs its entire potential against foreigners. When one adds to this the unequalled financial power of the GRU, vastly in excess of that of the KGB, it becomes clear why the most outstanding operations of Soviet intelligence have been mounted not by the KGB but by the GRU.

The minimum number of staff for any GRU undercover residency is two – the resident and a combined radio/cipher officer. Such a theoretical minimum exists also for the other organisations, the KGB and the Ministry of Foreign Affairs. Theoretically the Soviet colony in a very small country may consist of six people, three of whom, the ambassador and two residents, are diplomats, and the other three radio/cipher officers. Each of the three branches of the Soviet colony has its own enciphering machine and completely independent channel of communication with Moscow. Equally, each has its own boss in Moscow—the Minister of Foreign Affairs, the chairman of the KGB or the head of the GRU. Supreme arbitration between them can only be carried out in the Central Committee, which in its turn has an interest in fanning the flames of discord between the three organisations. The Central Committee has the right to recall any ambassador or resident and this same Central Committee has to decide questions as to which slots, and how many, should be accorded to each of the three organisations. This is a difficult task, as the Committee must not offend the KGB on questions of security, on the shadowing of its own diplomats above all, nor must it offend the GRU, for without the acquisition of data on present-day technology the quality of the Soviet Army would remain static. Finally it must not offend the 'clean ones'. They also must have a sufficient complement to serve as a screen for the dark activities of the two residencies.

This is why Soviet embassies, consulates, trade representations and so on grow and multiply and swell. As the residency grows, the resident acquires several deputies in place of the one he had at first. The number of radio/cipher officers increases. A technical services group is organised, an operational group, a tech-ops group, a radio monitoring station on the networks of the police and counter-intelligence. The number of operational officers engaged directly in recruiting and running agents increases. In the very biggest residencies of the GRU, such as that in New York, there may be from seventy to eighty officers. Medium-sized residencies like that in Rome would contain between thirty and forty officers. All officers on the staff of a residency are divided into three categories – operational staff, technical-operational staff and technical staff. The operational staff are those officers who are directly concerned with recruiting and running agents. In the operational staff are included residents, deputy residents and operational officers. To the technical-operations staff belong those officers who are directly concerned with and responsible for the production of intelligence, but who do not have personal contact with agents, nor often with foreigners at all. These are radio/cipher officers, officers of the technical services and operational technical services and the operators of the radio monitoring post. To the technical staff belong chauffeurs, guards and accountants.

The Resident

He is the senior representative of the GRU in any given place, and answerable only to the head of the GRU and the Central

Committee. He is the boss of all GRU officers and has the right to send any of them, including his own deputies, out of the country immediately. In this case he does not even have to justify his decision, even in front of the head of the GRU and the Central Committee. The resident is completely responsible for security, both as regards the work of each of his individual officers and recruited agents, and the security of the residency as a whole. He is chosen from among the most experienced officers and as a rule must have a minimum of three to five years of successful work as an operational officer and three to five years as the deputy resident before his appointment. A resident in a large residency will hold the military rank of major-general, in medium and small residencies that of colonel. This does not mean that a lieutenant-colonel cannot be appointed resident, but then, according to the GRU system, he will be paid a full colonel's or major-general's salary and, if he copes successfully, will have to fill posts commensurate with the higher rank. He is not afterwards permitted to return to a post ordinarily filled by a lieutenant-colonel.

The deputy resident serves as the resident's assistant and assumes his responsibilities when he is absent. He undertakes the duties given to him by the resident and carries on recruiting work in the same way as all other operational officers. Frequently a deputy resident heads teams of officers working in one or another specialised field. Sometimes the resident himself supervises the most experienced operational officers and the deputy residents the younger, less experienced officers. In some very large residencies, and also sometimes where there is great activity on the part of GRU illegals, there is a post called deputy resident for illegals. The undercover residency and the illegal residency are completely separate and the undercover residency has no idea how many illegals there are, or where or how they work. At the same time, on instructions from the Centre, the undercover residency continually gives them help and support, placing money and passports in dead-letter boxes, emptying dead-letter boxes for them, studying conditions and clarifying certain important questions. Very often the undercover residency is used to rescue illegals.

The military rank of any deputy resident is full colonel. At the same time the same rules apply as apply to residents. The deputy resident may be a lieutenant-colonel or even a major; however, from the administrative and financial points of view he is a full colonel with full rights.

The Operational Officer

This is a GRU officer who carries out the recruitment of agents, runs them and through them receives or acquires the secret documents and samples of weaponry and military technology. Every operational officer from the moment of his arrival in the country is obliged to recruit a minimum of one agent, as well as often having to take charge of one or two other secret agents who have previously been recruited by his predecessors. He must keep these agents and increase their productivity. An identical burden is placed on the deputy resident at the same time as he is fulfilling the obligations of a deputy. This system is applied in all small residencies. In medium-sized residencies, the resident himself may take a direct interest in recruitment or not as he wishes. The residents of very large residencies are exempted from personal recruitment.

Alongside his recruitment work, the operational officer carries on with the acquisition of intelligence material by all possible means. He converses with foreigners, travels around the country and reads the press avidly. However, the GRU's over-riding view is that recruitment work is the most important part of an officer's duty, and it calls it number one (in addition to certain other colloquial words). All other work – support and the performing of operations for others, however important – is known as zero. One may be added to zero if a 'zero' agent manages to recruit a foreigner, in which case he becomes a '10', which is clearly the best number to be. For this reason an operational officer who has been abroad for three years and not recruited a single agent, even if he has achieved outstanding success in collecting the most interesting intelligence material, is considered to be idle. According to the standards of the GRU, he has sat for three years doing absolutely nothing and therefore hardly merits consideration for another overseas posting.

The military rank of an operational officer is lieutenant-colonel or colonel but in practice he may be a major (as I was) or captain, or even a senior lieutenant. If he is successful in his recruitment work he stays on at this level receiving automatic promotion according to the length of time served. If he does not manage to recruit any agents, he is deprived of all his colonel's privileges and again becomes an ordinary senior lieutenant or captain and has to compete for promotion in the ordinary way, as automatic promotion is not granted to unsuccessful officers.

The military ranks prescribed for undercover residencies are also applicable for illegal residencies, with the sole difference that the illegal resident may be a major-general having many fewer people under his command than the resident of the undercover residency.

The Radio/Cipher Officer

Although he is an officer of technical operational staff, and his military rank is not usually higher than that of major, the radio/cipher officer is the second most important person in the residency. He is not only responsible for cipher matters, the storage and use of ciphers and cipher machines, but also for the transmission and reception of enciphered cables and the storage of all secret documentation in the residency. The radio/cipher officer possesses all the secrets of the residency and since he deciphers communications from Moscow he knows the news even earlier than the resident. Nobody, including the ambassador and the KGB resident, at any time or under any pretext has the right of access to his room. They do not even have the right to know the number and types of cipher machines installed there. These restrictions also apply to GRU deputy residents. Even during periods when the resident is away and the deputy resident is acting for him he does not have the right to go into the radio/cipher operator's room or to ask him any specific questions which have a bearing on his work. Only the resident may exercise any control over the cipher officer, and he pays for the privilege because the cipher officer is the only man in the residency who is entitled to communicate with Moscow without the knowledge of the resident. He can send a cable containing an adverse report about the resident of which the resident himself will know nothing. It is the duty of the cipher officer to exercise silent watch over the behaviour of the resident, and if there is any shortcoming he must report it. In small residencies, where there is only one radio/cipher officer, only the resident may replace him should he become incapacitated for any reason. If both the resident and the cipher officer should become incapacitated at the same time then the deputy resident and the whole residency will remain completely cut off from the Centre. Naturally the ambassador's and the KGB's channels of communication can be used, but only in order to inform the GRU in a very general way. It is natural therefore that great care is taken of cipher officers (this is just as true of the KGB as the GRU). Draconian living conditions are imposed on all cipher officers. They are only allowed to live in official Soviet embassy accommodation guarded around the clock. Neither the cipher officer nor his wife is allowed to leave the guarded territory independently or unaccompanied. They are at all times led by an officer who enjoys diplomatic immunity. Neither the officer nor his wife is allowed near places where foreigners are to be found. Even if these foreigners are Bulgarians or Mongolians and are on guarded territory belonging to a Soviet embassy, the restriction remains in force. The cipher officer is not allowed in the same room with them even though he may be silent and in the company of his resident. He and his family must have a diplomatic escort on their journey out from the Soviet Union and on their return. During the time of his assignment abroad, he is forbidden all leave. It is easy to see why cipher officers are not posted abroad for longer than two years.

Of course those cipher officers who have served their whole lives on the territory of the Soviet Union deeply envy those who have had postings abroad, no matter where; and those who have been abroad will give their right arms to get another posting abroad, no matter where – Calcutta, Shanghai or Beirut. They will agree to any conditions, any climate, any restrictions on their family lives, for they have learnt with their mother's milk the rule that overseas life is always better than in the Soviet Union.

Technical Services (TS) Officer

They are concerned with electronic intelligence from the premises of official Soviet premises, embassies, consulates, and so on. Basic targets are the telecommunications apparatus of the government,

diplomatic wireless communications, and military channels of communication. By monitoring radio transmissions, secret and cipher,
technical services groups not only obtain interesting information
but also cover the system of governmental communications, subordination of the different components of the state and the military
structure.

The military ranks of technical services officers are major and
lieutenant-colonel.

Radio Monitoring Station Officers

In contradistinction to TS officers, these are concerned with monitoring the radio networks of the police and security services. The
technical services and the radio monitoring station are two different
groups, independent of each other, both controlled by the resident.
The difference between them is that the technical services work in
the interests of the Centre, trying to obtain state secrets, but the
monitoring station works only in the interests of the residency trying to determine where in the city police activity is at its highest at
a given moment and thus where operations may be mounted and
where they should not be mounted. Groups for the study of operational conditions are made up of the most junior officers who
will eventually become operational officers and be sent out on independent recruitment work. These are small groups who continually
study the local press and police activities, endeavouring to obtain by
means of isolated snippets a general picture of the police work in a
given city and country. Besides their scanning of police reports for an
ultimate overview, they also minutely study and analyse, for example,
the numbers of police vehicles which appear in newspaper pictures
or the surnames of police officers and detectives. Sometimes this
painstaking work brings unexpected results. In one country a keen
journalist on a small newspaper reported a police plan to install secret
television cameras in order to survey the most highly populated parts
of the city; this was enough for the GRU to become interested and
to take corresponding measures. Within a month the GRU resident
was able to say with conviction that he was fully informed with regard to the police system of control by television and this enabled the
whole residency successfully to avoid traps laid for them for several

years. The military ranks of officers of these groups are senior lieutenant and captain.

The Operational Technical Group

This is concerned with the repair and maintenance of photographic
apparatus, photocopying equipment and the like. At the disposal of
the group there are dead-letter boxes of all types, radio transmission stations, SW (secret writing) materials, microphotography and
micropantography. The officers of this group are always on hand to
give the necessary explanations to operational officers and to instruct them on the use of this or that instrument or method. These
officers continually monitor television programmes and collect useful items on video tape, giving to Moscow material it could not get
from any other source. The officers of the group, together with the
officers of the group for the study of operational conditions, are
widely used for the security of agent operations, the carrying out of
counter-surveillance, signals organisation, dead-letter box operations
and so on.

Technical Personnel

Only the very largest residencies contain technical personnel. Drivers are only allocated to residents who hold the rank of general.
However, many generals, in an effort to be indistinguishable from
other diplomats, dispense with the services of drivers. The military
rank of a driver is an ensign. However, sometimes an operational officer is to be found in the guise of a driver and he, of course, has a
much superior rank. This is a widespread method of deception, for
who would pay attention to a driver?

Some residencies, especially those in countries where attacks
on the embassy cannot be excluded, have a staff of guards besides
the KGB guards who are responsible for the external protection of
the building. The GRU internal security guards consist of young
Spetsnaz officers in the rank of lieutenant or senior lieutenant. The
internal security guards of the residency may be deployed at the
request of the resident in countries where KGB attempts to pen
etrate the GRU get out of hand. The internal security guards answer

directly to the resident or his deputy. Naturally they do not take part in agent handling operations.

An accountant, in the rank of captain or major, is employed only in those residencies where the normal monthly budget exceeds one million dollars. In other cases the financial affairs are the concern of one of the deputy residents.

★

In our examination of the undercover residency, we have naturally to examine its cover, the official duties used by KGB and GRU officers to camouflage their secret activities. Without exaggeration it may be said that any official duty given to Soviet citizens abroad may be used to mask officers of intelligence organisations: as ambassadors and drivers, consuls and guards, dancers, writers, artists, simple tourists, guides and stewardesses, heads of delegations and simple section heads, UN employees and priests, intelligence officers conceal their true functions. Any person who has the right of official entry and exit from the Soviet Union may be used for intelligence tasks, and the vast majority of these are in fact only occupied in intelligence work. Some types of cover provide better possibilities, some worse. Some are used more by the GRU, some more by the KGB. Let us look at the basic ones.

The embassy is used to an equal extent by both organisations. Both residents and their deputies are in possession of massive amounts of information which would expose them to an unacceptably high risk of arrest. For this reason the KGB resident and his colleague from the GRU, and usually their deputies too, are bearers of diplomatic passports, that is, they work officially in the embassies. Other officers of both organisations give themselves out as embassy diplomats too. They all prefer to concern themselves with technological and scientific questions, and questions of transport and communications; they are rarely found in cultural sections. The consulate is entirely KGB. You will almost never find officers of the GRU there and only very rarely genuine diplomats. This is because all exit and entry from and to the Soviet Union is in the hands of the KGB. KGB officers in the consulate issue visas, and the frontier forces of the KGB then control them later on. Every aspect of immigration and of flight and defection has some connection with consular affairs, which therefore rank extremely high in the KGB's sphere of interest. So it follows that the percentage of KGB officers in consulates is unusually high, even by Soviet standards. (There do exist very rare instances of GRU officers working in consulates. The KGB only agrees to this on the grounds of practical considerations, and so that it should not appear to be too one-sided an organisation.)

Aeroflot, the Soviet civil airline, is the exclusive domain of the GRU. This can be explained by the fact that aviation technology is of extreme interest to the Soviet armaments industry, and there is huge scope for any Aeroflot employee to inform himself about the progress of the West: international exhibitions, meetings with representatives of the leading aviation and space corporations, perfectly justifiable meetings with representatives of firms producing aviation electronics, oils, lubricants, fuels, high-tension materials, heat isolators and aero-engines. Usually the firms which produce civil aircraft also produce military aircraft and rockets, and in this field lie the GRU's richest pickings. Happily, those officers whom the GRU selects at advanced aviation institutes for work in Aeroflot do not need lengthy specialist instruction. Sometimes Soviet military and civil aircraft have identical parts. KGB officers are only rarely employed at Aeroflot, and then for the same reasons as the GRU in consular affairs. The merchant navy is almost identical, the only difference being that the officers there are selected to study cruisers and submarines and not strategic aviation. An organisation of exceptional importance to both services is the Trade Representation, that is the organ of the Ministry of External Trade. Literally swarming with KGB and GRU officers, this organisation provides exceptional access to business people whom both strive to exploit for their own ends. Representation in Tass, APN, *Pravda* and *Izvestia* are almost forbidden ground for the GRU. Even the KGB in this field has very narrow powers. Press matters are very carefully kept in the Central Committee's own hands, therefore KGB officers and officers of the GRU do not occupy key posts in these organisations. This does not mean of course that their secret activities suffer in any way.

Intourist is in the KGB's hands, so much so that it is not just an organisation strongly influenced by the KGB, but an actual branch of the KGB. Beginning with the construction of hotels and the putting of advertisements in the papers, and ending with the recruitment of foreigners in those same hotels, it is all run entirely by the KGB. GRU officers are found in Intourist, but rarely. There does exist, however, one rule which admits of no exceptions. Anything to do with the military attachés is staffed exclusively by officers of the GRU. Here there are no genuine diplomats, nor KGB. The naval, military and air attachés are regarded by the GRU as its particular brand of cover. In the West one is accustomed to see in these people not spies but military diplomats, and one assumes that this has spread to one's Soviet colleagues. This deep misapprehension is fully exploited by the GRU. Whenever you talk to a Soviet military attaché, remember always that before you stands at the very least an operational officer of an undercover residency who is faced with the problem of recruiting foreigners and who, if he does not recruit a single foreigner, sees all his other work become insignificant and all his hopes of a shining career crash to the ground. Look into his eyes and ask him how much longer he has to serve in this hospitable country and if in his answer you perceive a note of anguish, then be on your guard, for he will recruit you if he can. But perhaps he is happy with life and his eyes express pleasure. This means he has recruited one of your fellow-countrymen. Possibly there even stands in front of you a deputy resident or the GRU resident himself. Fear him and be careful of him. He is dangerous. He is experienced and cunning like an old hand should be. This is not his first time abroad, and that means he has already chalked up a significant number of successful recruits.

★

Every GRU officer in an undercover residency, whatever his official duties may be, and under whatever cover he masquerades, has his place in the general structure of the secret hierarchy. What we see in daily life is only the performance the GRU wishes to show us. Internal relations in an undercover residency have no bearing whatsoever on external, official ranks. Military ranks play an insignificant role. The important role is the actual job of the officer in the residency. There have been cases where residents with an eye to cover have occupied completely insignificant posts within embassies. At the same time the resident remains the resident and his authority is unshakeable. Within the residency he remains the strict, tyrannical, frequently wilful boss who during his briefings will frequently attack the military attachés — even though in his life as seen by the outside world he plays the part of doorman for those same attachés. The second most important person, the deputy resident, may only be a lieutenant-colonel with operational officers who are colonels but this does not prevent him from talking to them as he would to captains or lieutenants. They are only operational officers, while the GRU has decreed that he, a lieutenant-colonel, is better than them, full colonels though they may be, and has given him full powers to dispose of them and order them about. Official cover again plays absolutely no part. An operational officer may assume the official duty of assistant to a military attaché or military attaché himself, but still have the deputy resident as his own personal driver. The deputy resident is no way suffers from this. His situation is analogous to that of the Sicilian waiter who, off duty, is senior in rank to the restaurant owner within the Mafia hierarchy.

All operational officers are legal equals, from senior lieutenants to full colonels. Their seniority in the residency, however, is established by the resident exclusively on the basis of the quantity and quality of their recruitments. Recruitment work is the sole criterion for all GRU officers, regardless of age, rank or official duties. Their relations with each other in the residency might be compared with the relationships existing between fighter pilots in time of war. They also, in their own circle, pay little attention to length of service or military rank. Their criterion of respect for a man is the number of enemy aircraft he has shot down, and a lieutenant who has shot down ten aircraft may patronisingly slap on the shoulder a major who has not shot down a single aircraft. The attitude of the operational staff engaged in recruitment work to other officers may be summed up by comparison with the attitude of the fliers and the ground staff at a fighter base: 'I fly in the sky and you shovel shit.' The only exception to this attitude is the radio/cipher officer, to whom all show the greatest respect, because he knows much more about intelligence matters concerning the residency than the deputy resident.

★

Let us take a typically large residency as an example and examine it. Everything is factual. The resident is a Major-General A and his official cover (relatively unimportant), is First Secretary, Embassy. Directly beneath him are a group of five radio/cipher officers, three very experienced operational officers (one of whom runs an agent group, and two others who run especially valuable agent-sources), and four deputy residents. They are:

Colonel B, cover Deputy Trade Representative. He has twelve GRU officers below him, all working in the Trade Representation. He is in contact with one agent. One of his officers runs an agent group of three agents. Another is in contact with two agents and a third officer has one agent. The remaining officers have as yet no agents.

Lt-Colonel C, cover Assistant to the Naval Attaché. He has many operational officers beneath him, two of whom work in the Merchant Navy Representation, three in Aeroflot, five in the Embassy and ten in the departments of the Military, Naval and Air Attachés. All three of the military departments are considered to be a diplomatic unit independent from each other and from the Embassy. However, in this case, all officers entering the three military departments including the three attachés are beneath one assistant military attaché. The deputy resident is in contact with one agent. Twelve other operational officers subordinate to him have one agent each. The remainder have acquaintances who are to be recruited within one to two years. In addition to his agent-running work, this deputy resident is responsible for information work in the whole residency.

Colonel D, cover First Secretary, Embassy (deputy resident for illegals). This deputy resident has no agent and does not carry out recruitment work. He has no officers beneath him, but when he is carrying out operations in the interests of illegals, he can make use of any of the best officers of the first and second groups.

Lt-Colonel E, cover Second Secretary, Embassy. He is in contact with one agent. One operational officer is subordinate to him, disguised as the military attaché's driver, and this officer runs an agent group. In addition, this deputy resident controls the following: one technical service group (six officers), one group for the study of operational conditions (four officers), one group of operational technique (two officers), the radio monitoring station (three officers), five officers of the internal security guards for the residency and one accounts officer.

★

In all there are sixty-seven officers in the residency, of whom forty-one are operational staff, twenty operational technological staff and six technical staff. The residency has thirty-six agents, of whom twenty-five work independently of each other.

In some cases part of the undercover residency, under the command of one of the deputy residents, functions in another city permanently detached from the basic forces of the main residency. This is true, for example, of Holland, where the undercover residency is located in The Hague but part of the residency is in Amsterdam. Such an arrangement complicates work to a considerable degree but in the opinion of the GRU it is better to have two small residencies than one big one. In this case any failure in one of the residencies does not reflect on the activities of the other. Everywhere it is possible, the GRU endeavours to organise new, independent residencies. For this it has to observe two basic conditions: the presence of official Soviet diplomatic representation – an embassy, consulate, military attaché's department, military communications mission or a permanent UN mission; and the presence of an officially registered radio station in direct contact with Moscow. Where these two conditions obtain, residencies can be quickly organised, even the very smallest possible, consisting of two men but independent and self-contained.

Apart from the security angle, this practice also ensures parallelism, as the GRU can control one resident by means of another. Such possibilities are open to Soviet intelligence in many countries. For example, in Paris there is one of the most expansionist undercover

residencies of the GRU. Independent of it in Marseilles there is another, smaller residency. Their performance is vastly enhanced by the
fierce competition between them. In West Germany the GRU has
been able to create five residencies. Wherever there is official Soviet
diplomatic representation with radio transmission, there is also an
undercover residency of the GRU. In many cases there is also an undercover residency of the KGB. But while the residencies of the GRU
are organised in any official mission – civil, military or mixed – those
of the KGB are not. In Marseilles, New York, Amsterdam, Geneva
and Montreal the Soviet missions are clearly civil, and in all these
cities there are undercover residencies of both KGB and GRU. But
where the mission is clearly military, as for example the Soviet observation mission in West Germany, the KGB may not have a residency.
This also applies to the numerous missions of Soviet military advisers in developing countries. The KGB presence there is only for the
maintenance of security among the genuine military advisers.

In speaking about the undercover residency we must not forget
to mention another category of people participating in espionage
activities – co-opted personnel. These are Soviet citizens abroad who
are not officers of the GRU or the KGB, but fulfil a number of tasks set
them by these organisations. The co-opted person may be of any rank
from doorman to ambassador and he carries out very different tasks,
from studies of the foreigners surrounding him to clearing dead-letter
boxes. The KGB has always been interested in the exploitation of co-
opted persons; following the principle of 'don't stick your own neck
out if you can get somebody else to stick it out for you'. The GRU is
not so keen, using co-opted persons only in exceptional cases. Its guid-
ing principle is: 'don't trust even your best friend with your motor car,
girlfriend – or agent'. The rewards for a co-opted person are monetary
ones which, unlike the basic salary, are not subject to tax. Usually in
every embassy, consulate and trade representation, out of every ten
'clean' officials, seven are co-opted onto the KGB staff, one onto the
GRU staff; only the remaining two are clean. Either they are complete
idiots, or the sons of members of the Central Committee whom wild
horses could not force to have anything to do with intelligence. In
other words, in Soviet official institutions, it is a very, very tricky matter indeed to meet a man who has no connections with intelligence.

Chapter Three

Agents

In present-day Soviet intelligence terminology the term 'agent' has only one meaning. An agent is a foreigner recruited by Soviet intelligence and carrying out secret tasks on its behalf. All agents, irrespective of the group or section of the GRU to which they belong, are divided into two groups: the basic agent and the supplementary agent. Basic agents fall into four categories: they are residents or group leaders; they are providers of information; they are executive agents whose main task is to kill; or they are recruiting agents. In the supplementary group are wireless operators, legalising agents, documentalists, the owners of safe houses, addresses, telephones and radio transmission points.

Head Agents

Head agents are the leaders of agent groups and agent residents. Head agents are selected from the most experienced agents available, men and women who have had long years of service and have given proof of their devotion to duty. They are invested with wide powers and possess significant financial independence. In cases where the organisation entrusted to them collapses, the head agent must take the decision to do away with unwanted people who pose a threat to it. In this and other emergencies he can always count on the full support of the GRU.

The difference between the group leader and the agent resident is that the group leader may take a whole range of important decisions concerning the group entrusted to him, but he may not recruit agents at all. The agent resident has a wider range of interests, the most important being recruitment. The group leader may be subordinate to the residency, to the illegal, undercover or agent residency or directly to the Centre, but the agent resident may only be subordinate to the Centre.

Sources

These are agents who directly obtain secret information, documents or samples of military technology and weaponry. In the recruitment of such people, it is first and foremost their access to political, military, technological and other secrets which is taken into account. It is clearly unnecessary to recruit an officer from the Ministry of Defence if one can recruit his secretary. In other words, the GRU has contact with people occupying relatively unimportant posts but with possibly greater knowledge than their superiors. With this in mind, apart from secretaries, the people of special interest to the GRU are workers in printing and typing offices which produce secret documents, cipher officers, diplomatic couriers, computer operators, communications clerks, draughtsmen and other technical personnel.

Executive Agents

These are agents recruited to carry out assassinations, diversions or sabotage. The recruitment of executive agents is not usually carried out by the central GRU, but by the local organs of the GRU—the military district departments. Sometimes even strategic intelligence needs similar specialists, but in smaller number.

Executive agents are recruited from criminal elements and from that band of naturally brutish characters who, with passing time, become accustomed to executing any orders they are given. Frequently agents who have been acting as providers of information are transferred by both the strategic and operational branches of the GRU to the category of executive agent, in cases where they may have lost their access.

Agent Recruiters

These are the most devoted and thoroughly tested agents, people who either never had access or who have lost it. As their name suggests, the GRU uses them solely for the recruitment of new agents. The most successful will eventually become group leader or sometimes agent resident.

Agent Legalisers

These are subsidiary agents. They work in the interests of illegals and as a rule are recruited and run only by illegals. Candidates for this category of agents are sought among officials of the police and passport departments, consular clerks, customs and immigration officials, and small employers of labour. Agent legalisers are subjected to especially thorough vetting, because the fate of illegals is entrusted to them. When a Soviet illegal arrives in a country the task of the legalising agent is to ensure the issue of documents by making the necessary entries in the registration books and to ensure that the illegal is in possession of the necessary documentation.

In the history of the GRU quite a few priests carrying falsified documents and registers of baptism and death have given immense service to illegals who, on the basis of false entries, have been able to obtain the necessary documents. A similar role to that of the legalising agent is played by the *documentation agents*. These are recruited by the undercover residency and their job is to obtain passports, driving licences and samples of official police forms. In contradistinction to the legalising agents, documentation agents do not have any direct contact with illegals. Although they obtain tens and sometimes hundreds, even thousands of passports, they have no direct knowledge of how and when the GRU is going to use them. Frequently the GRU uses the passports obtained through the good offices of documentation agents only as a sample for the preparation of similar falsified copies. Documentation agents may be recruited from among criminal classes who are occupied with the forging and selling of documents on the black market and also from clerks concerned with the production, inventory, storage and issue of passports. Frequently documentation agents have successfully worked among poor students, persuading them, for a financial consideration, to lose their passports.

Couriers

These are supplementary agents engaged in transporting agent materials over state frontiers. Obviously it is not necessary to employ special couriers to transport the material into the Soviet Union or its satellites.

The basic flow of agent material which is not subject to particular suspicion goes from countries with hard regimes into countries with

more soft regimes. In the opinion of the GRU, an opinion fortified
by the experience of many years, the hardest country is Great Britain,
followed by France, the United States, the Federal Republic of
Germany, Belgium and Holland. As soft countries the GRU includes
Finland, Ireland and Austria among others.

The GRU also makes very wide use of countries of the Third
World for this purpose, and couriers may sometimes make very long
journeys before the material finally arrives in the hands of the GRU.
Examples are known of material obtained in the United States going
first to Latin America, then to Africa and only from Africa being conveyed to the Soviet Union. In recruiting couriers, the GRU pays particular attention to the drivers and guards of long-distance trains, commercial travellers and sailors of merchant fleets. When hi-jacking of
aircraft became more frequent and controls at airports became stricter,
the GRU virtually gave up recruiting the crews of airliners. If it uses
these at all, it is only for transporting small-sized non-metallic objects.

The Owner of a Safe House or Flat

He is a supplementary agent occupying a position of great trust,
usually recruited from among house-owners, concierges and hotel
owners, in a word, all those who possess not one but several flats or
dwelling places. The term 'safe flat' should be understood not only
in its generally accepted meaning but also as a well-equipped cellar,
attic, garage or store. For safe flats the GRU selects quiet secluded
places where they may want to be able to hide a man sometimes
for a length of several months; to carry out meetings, briefings and
de-briefings; to change clothes and change appearances; and to hide
stolen materials and photograph stolen documents. The owner of a
safe house or flat is known in the colloquial language of the GRU by
the abbreviation 'KK'.

The Safe Address Owner

He is an agent who receives and transmits secret messages for the
GRU, usually recruited from among those people who receive co-
pious correspondence from abroad; the work is normally restricted to inhabitants of 'soft' countries. Sources who have obtained

information and intelligence in hard countries send letters in SW to these addresses and the owners transmit the correspondence to officers of the undercover residency. One interesting aspect of recruitment is that the GRU prefers middle-aged people who would not be affected by general mobilisation in the country, so that the chain of communication is not interrupted.

The possessors of secret telephones and, more recently, teleprinters are recruited by the same rules applied to the owners of secret addresses. In GRU language these types of agent networks and their possessors are known by the abbreviations 'KA', 'KT', 'KTP'.

The owners of transmitting points are used for transmitting agent materials within the limits of one city or area. Usually they are street sellers in small kiosks, stalls or paper stalls. An agent who has acquired intelligence will stop and hand over the material to the owner. Hours later, sometimes days, GRU officers will visit the stall to collect the material and hand over money for the agents together with new instructions. This avoids direct contact between the GRU and the agent. Increased security might mean the source agent using a dead-letter box which the stall holder will empty, not knowing who has filled it. The GRU will announce the dead-letter box's whereabouts to the transmitting point only after it has been filled. A different one will be used for each operation, and so even if the police discover that the GRU has a special interest in the small shop or stall and subsequently establishes that this stall serves as a transmitting point, it will still be very difficult to discover the source agent. To mount a surveillance operation in the neighbourhood of the dead-letter box is impossible since the transmitting point only acquires its location after it has been filled; the agent himself has disappeared long before. The transmitting point is known by the abbreviation 'PP'.

Chapter Four

Agent Recruiting

Agent recruiting is the most important task of both strategic and operational intelligence. No real problems can be solved without agent penetration in basic government, military and technological centres of the enemy.

In the previous chapter we examined the types of secret agents and also the various differences between them. It would not be an exaggeration to say that any citizen of the West, having been recruited by the GRU, may be used very effectively for intelligence purposes, some for the acquisition of secret documents, some for assassinating people, and some for the transporting of agent materials. No citizen of any age and either sex would be idle for long once he or she fell into the hands of the GRU. Nevertheless, basic importance is attached to the provider of information. Long experience has persuaded the GRU that it is essential above all to recruit sources, and only after the GRU has acquired through these sources all possible material may the source himself be used for other purposes, as a recruiter, head agent or supplementary agent. The GRU is convinced that a former source who is now working, for example, as the owner of a transmitting point will never on his own initiative go to the police; but the same cannot be said of agents who have never provided secrets for the GRU, who have not had firm contacts with them. The search for suitable candidates is implemented at the same time in certain different ways: the scrupulous collection of information on persons of interest to the GRU including government institutions for staffs, military bases, design bureaux and people connected with these targets; the study of all foreigners without exception who have any contacts at all with officers of the GRU; and the gradual widening of circles of acquaintances among foreigners. If an operational officer has a hundred acquaintances, one of these must surely be a potential provider of information which will be of interest.

A candidate for recruitment must fulfil the following conditions: he must have agent potential, that is he must be in the position to provide information of real use to the GRU, either to steal or copy secrets, to communicate secret information by word of mouth, or to recruit new agents. There must exist motives by means of which he may be recruited – displeasure with the regime or other political motives, personal financial problems, or private motives like a desire for revenge on somebody or secret crimes which he is trying to hide. It is desirable that he be sympathetic to communism without being a communist. Communist parties everywhere have been compromised to a certain extent by their contacts with the KGB and the GRU, and it is always recommended that agents recruited from communist parties should leave the party.

After the selection of a candidate for recruitment, the second stage – tracing and vetting – commences. Details are collected about the candidate, details which may be obtained through reference books, telephone directories and the press; the task of obtaining all available information about the candidate may well be given to other agents. The GRU may equally want a surveillance on him to collect extra data about his daily life. This process sometimes gives very gratifying results. Up to now the person himself does not suspect that the GRU exists and he has had no contact with its representatives, but it already has a considerable wealth of detail on him. Subsequently the GRU enters the process of cultivation, which consists in a further definition of motives which will be used in the actual recruitment of the person. It also tries to exacerbate his weaknesses: for example, if the man experiences financial problems, the GRU will endeavour to make them worse. If he is displeased with the political regime, the GRU will endeavour to turn his displeasure into hatred. The cultivation process may be carried out after the establishment of an acquaintanceship with the candidate. The whole process, from the beginning of the search for a candidate to the completion of a cultivation period, normally extends for not less than a year; only after this does actual recruitment take place.

There are two principal methods of recruitment, the gradual approach and the crash approach. The crash approach is the highest class of agent work. The GRU may authorise the resident to mount such an operation only if the resident has been able to provide good arguments for the taking of such a risk. Quite a few examples are known of recruitment at the first meeting, of course following the secret cultivation which has gone on for many months. It was in this way that many American creators of the first atomic bomb were recruited. Their subsequent argument was that it was as a mark of protest against the bombing of the Japanese cities that they, on their own initiative, established contact with Soviet intelligence. However, for some reason they forgot to add that this contact had been established long before the first experiments with the bomb, when there was no cause for protest. They also evaded the question as to how several people, simultaneously and independently from one another, established contact with the undercover residency of the GRU in Canada, but not with the undercover residency of the KGB in Mexico, for example.

The crash approach, or 'love at first sight' in GRU jargon, has a number of irrefutable advantages. Contact with the future agent takes place only once, instead of at meetings over many months, as is the case with the gradual approach. After the first contact the new-ly recruited agent will himself take action on his own security. He will never talk to his wife, or tell her that he has a charming friend in the Soviet military attaché who is also very interested in stamp collecting.

In the gradual approach method, this sort of thing happens very, very often. The candidate has as yet not felt the deadly grip of the GRU, has not yet understood what it wants from him. He still nour-ishes his illusions, and naturally he will not hide his good friendship with such charming people. However, the gradual approach method, despite its shortcomings, is frequently used. The fact is that the GRU is not always, indeed not even in the majority of cases, able to col-lect a sufficient amount of material about the candidate without his knowledge to prepare him sufficiently for recruitment. In many cases it is necessary to establish contact and to use each meeting with the candidate to study his motives and to carry out vetting and cultivation.

Having established contact, the operational officer tries by ev-ery possible method to avoid 'blowing' the candidate; that is, he tries to hide the connection from the police, from friends and ac-quaintances of the man himself, and also from his own fellow coun-trymen. The only people who should know anything about an agent and therefore about candidates for recruitment are the resi-dent, the deputy resident and of course the cipher officer and the Centre - nobody else. In order that he should not blow the candidate from the very first meeting, the operational officer will try to carry out meetings in secluded restaurants, cafés, bars far from the place where the candidate lives and far from his place of work. At all costs he will try to avoid the candidate telephoning him either at home or in the embassy. He will try to avoid the candidate visiting Soviet official institutions and places where Soviet people gather together. He will decline invitations to meet the candidate's family or visit his home. (The particular pretexts I used were that my office was far too busy, or I was never there, so the candidate would not ring; at home, I would tell him, there was a small baby who slept badly. Of course, in order to appear serious, I had to give him the telephone numbers with my business card.) After the acquaintanceship has ripened, the GRU officer will try to make every subsequent meeting as interesting and useful as possible for the candidate. If they exchange postage stamps, then the Soviet, by apparent mistake or out of friendship, will give the future agent a very valuable stamp. The officer may then ask for a very innocent and insignificant favour from the man and pay him very generously for it. During this stage the most important thing is that the future agent becomes accustomed to being asked favours and fulfilling them accurately. It does not matter what sort of favours or services. Maybe he will be asked to accept at his address and forward to the officers letters ostensibly from his mistress, or to buy a complete set of telephone directories and give them to the officer as if he did not know how or where this could be done. By degrees the tasks become more complicated, but the payment for them grows equally. Perhaps he will be asked to acquire in his name some works of reference which are not on sale and are distributed only on signature, or he will be asked to talk about and describe his friends who work with him. In many cases the actual recruitment proposal is never made, as the candidate gradually becomes an agent of the GRU without having fully realised it. He may consider that he is simply doing his business and doing favours for a good friend. Then, much to his surprise, the man will one day find that all ways of extricating himself have been cut off, and that he is deeply ensnared in espionage work. After he has become aware of this for himself, the GRU informs him what the affair is all about and there begins a new stage. The tasks become more serious but the payment for them gradually decreases. This is done on the pretext of his own security. What can he do? Go on strike?

As for GRU illegals, they basically use the first two methods. The work of illegals of course is made easier by the obvious simplification of the search for candidates and their tracing and vetting. Since they

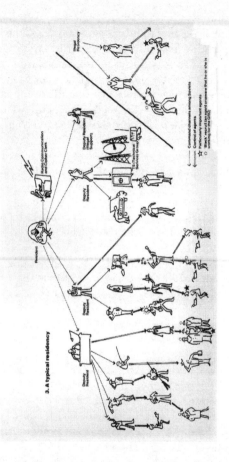

3. A typical residency

very often play the part of bona fide business people they come into frequent contact with the owners of firms producing military material, and by means of proposing advantageous deals, they gradually attract these people to play the part of agents. There is another very important factor. Illegals hardly ever recruit in the name of Soviet intelligence. They always assume another guise. In Japan, for example, they may pass themselves off as American industrial spies, in Northern Ireland as an organisation going in for terrorist activities against the English military presence, in Arab countries as anti-Zionists. In countries with dictatorial regimes GRU illegals recruit people in the name of anti-government organisations carrying on the underground struggle against tyranny. A method often used by illegals is to pass themselves off as supporters of separatist movements. It is only necessary for the illegal to know some of the important political views in order to be able to adopt them for himself and begin recruiting. Sometimes such recruitments are implemented very quickly and without problems. 'We are representatives of such and such a liberation army, this or that red brigade. Can't you help us? If you can't we ask you not to let anybody know about our visit.' The candidate is then recruited in the name of an organisation for which he feels sympathy and he gratifies his conscience all his life with the thought that he is a revolutionary and defends ideals near to his heart, not even suspecting the existence of the GRU and its illegals. He is so full of pride that he has been selected for such secret work that he may not even tell those who think likewise about it.

There is one last method of recruiting. This is when a foreigner comes in and says, 'Please recruit me.' However strange it may seem, every year hundreds of such people come into Soviet embassies and the same answer awaits them all. 'This is a diplomatic representation and not an espionage centre. Be so kind as to leave the building or we will call the police.' The police are usually not called but the embassy staff chase the would-be agent out quickly. Even if the GRU (and the KGB, for that matter) is sure that the caller is not a young reporter anxious to publish a sensational article or somebody purporting to sell secret documents but really only selling some nonsense, how can they be sure that the caller is not a police agent who wants to know who in the embassy is concerned with secrets? …

That these 'walk-ins' are an extremely unpredictable form of recruitment is perhaps best illustrated by two examples, both of which occurred at the same residency in West Germany. An American sergeant came to one of the Soviet observation missions in West Germany (each of which is a GRU residency), bringing with him the block of a cipher machine used in one of the American bases. The sergeant announced that for a certain sum he could bring a second part of the machine and added that there could only be a deal on condition that the GRU would not subsequently attempt to recruit him. The residency immediately accepted both proposals. The sergeant got his money and an assurance that the GRU would forget all about him immediately after the deal was done.

The cipher machine which was obtained, or more accurately two of its basic blocks; enabled the technical services of the GRU to decipher thousands of American radio communications which had been intercepted earlier but remained undeciphered. They also enabled them to study the principles of cipher work in the American Army and in the armies of its allies and, by exploiting the American principles, to create more complete Soviet examples. What about the sergeant? Of course he was immediately recruited. ...

On another occasion a couple of years later an American major approached the same Soviet residency proposing to sell an American atomic artillery shell. In proof of his good intentions he handed over free of charge to the residency detailed plans of the atomic depots and instructions on checking procedures and standing orders for work with atomic equipment. These documents by themselves were of great value, although the major's main proposal was of vastly greater interest. The major announced that he would demand a substantial sum for the shell, and imposed the condition that the Soviet side, having studied the shell, must return it after two months. Some days later, the specialists of the GRU information service confirmed the genuineness and very great importance of the documents which had been acquired. The GRU leadership decided to buy the atomic shell and to pay the price demanded for it by the American. A number of the senior officers of the residency were called to Moscow and given a crash course in American atomic technology. A week later, on a dark rainy night in a clearing in the middle of a forest, two motor cars met. In one was the American major, in the other three operational officers. There were two more Soviet cars hidden nearby, ready to intervene if necessary. Many people did without sleep that night. The Soviet Consul dozed by his telephone, in full readiness to come tearing out to the wood and in the name of the Union of Soviet Socialist Republics to defend the military diplomats. On the orders of the Central Committee, many highly placed officials in the Ministry of Foreign Affairs and Tass were also on alert. Of course they did not know what was going on or where, but they were ready to announce to the world that the imperialists had mounted yet another provocation against the Soviet Union. In fact, the Tass and Ministry of Foreign Affairs announcements were already prepared. But everything went according to plan. The American and the three Soviets transferred the shell from one car to the other, and a thorough check was carried out. The operational officers knew beforehand the serial number, the level of radiation, the exact weight and the markings which would identify it as a genuine shell. All was as it should be. The Soviets handed over a briefcase full of banknotes to the American and agreed to meet in two months' time for the return of the shell. Once the shell was in the Soviet car with diplomatic number plates, it was tantamount to being on Soviet territory. The police could stop the car, but they did not have the right to search it nor remove anything from it. Diplomatic immunity is not to be trifled with. In the event nobody stopped the officers, and the car drove peacefully into the courtyard of the Soviet diplomatic mission. Later the shell was transported in a diplomatic container under armed guard to the Soviet Union.

The GRU chief joyfully informed the Central Committee of the successful outcome of the operation. 'Where is the bomb?' asked a voice on the telephone. 'We have it in GRU headquarters.' 'In Moscow!?' 'Yes.'

A long and largely unprintable tirade ensued, whose import was roughly as follows: 'And what happens if there is a little spring inside this shell and it explodes right in the middle of the Soviet capital and turns Moscow into Hiroshima?'

The GRU had worked out the whole operation with the maximum number of precautionary measures and the plan to acquire the shell had been confirmed by all departments from the chief to the general staff up to the Central Committee. However, nobody had foreseen the possibility that there could be a timed device in the shell and that the Central Committee, the Politburo, the KGB, the GRU, all the Ministers and departments of State, the general staff, all the Military Academies, all the principal design bureaus, in a word, everything which constitutes Soviet power, could be instantaneously destroyed. There was no answer. No defence was possible. One shell and the whole system could have gone up, because everybody and everything is controlled from Moscow. The possibility of such an occurrence had only been realised in the Central Committee when the shell was already in Moscow. Instead of the expected decoration, the GRU chief received a 'service incompetence note' – a strong warning that in the future even the most trivial mistake would lead to dismissal.

The shell was taken for the time being to the central aerodrome and a military transport aircraft speedily transported it to Novaya Zemlya. The shell did not explode. At the same time there was no guarantee that it would not explode while it was being dismantled and destroy the leading Soviet specialists who were working on it, so the dismantling was conducted in a special pavilion hurriedly constructed on the atomic testing ground. Preliminary work on the shell had already disquieted the Soviet specialists, as it was much more radioactive than it should have been. After protracted arguments and consultations, the shell was dismantled with the greatest possible care. Only then was it found that it was not a shell at all – but a beautifully executed copy.

The American major from the depot for atomic armaments had known to the last detail how to do this. He had taken a written-off practice shell or, as it is called, a 'standard weight equivalent', had painted it as a real shell and put on a corresponding marking and number. Inside the shell he had put some radioactive waste which he had obtained. Of course he was not able to regulate this to the extent that the level of radiation would conform to the level of radiation of a genuine shell, but this was not necessary. At the time when it was first checked after having been handed over to the operational officers, there had been no attempt to determine the exact level of radioactivity. The officers had only been interested to see whether there was radiation or not. After all that had happened the officers who had taken part in the operation, of course, received no decorations but at the same time they were not punished and neither was the GRU chief. The Special Commission of the General Staff and Central Committee established that the forgery had been very skilfully and thoroughly executed and that there had been little possibility of exposing it at the time of the hand-over. All the same the GRU was not happy about it. It began a search for the American major. The first attempts proved unsuccessful. It was established that he had been posted to the USA immediately after the sale of the forgery, and it would not be so easy to find him there. He had apparently known of the imminence of his posting and chosen his moment perfectly. Steps were taken to find him in the United States, and at the same time the GRU asked for permission to murder him from the Central Committee. However, the Central Committee turned down the request on the basis that the major was incredibly cunning and could well outwit the GRU a second time as he had outwitted them earlier. They were ordered to forget about the major and stop searching for him. Now, whenever a 'walk-in' appears at a Soviet embassy and suggests the purchase for an exorbitant price of technical documents of exceptional importance, GRU residents always remember the American major.

That it is extremely difficult to find real volunteers is a simple fact. It is much, much harder to discover a volunteer than an agent whom the GRU has spent a year and more in processing. But real volunteers, however warmly they may be welcomed, do not take into consideration another simple thing. The Soviet operational officer, having seen a great deal of the ugly face of communism, very frequently feels the utmost repulsion to those who sell themselves to it willingly. Even amongst those few who still believe in communism, the intelligence officer will make a great distinction between the agent he has recruited by using a whole arsenal of tricks and traps, and the volunteer. And when a GRU or KGB officer decides to break with his criminal organisation, something which fortunately happens quite often, the first thing he will do is try to expose the hated volunteer.

CHAPTER 3

SPY OPERATIONS — THE ATOM SPIES AND PENKOVSKY

The Vassiliev Notebooks

After the end of the Cold War and the collapse of the Soviet Union in 1991, the old Cold War intelligence agencies also disappeared, to be replaced by successor organizations including the FSB (which took over the KGB's internal security operations) and the SVR (which assumed its foreign intelligence role). The SVR decided to allow limited access to the KGB's archives to foreign publishers working with retired KGB operatives in a bid to raise its profile in the fragmenting world of post-Soviet intelligence. One of these, Alexander Vassiliev, compiled a series of notebooks which were later smuggled out of Russia and formed the basis of several books.

The notebooks concentrate on Soviet–American and Anglo–Soviet affairs, with a particular focus on the spies who stole America's atomic secrets. The Soviet code-name for the Manhattan Project, the American programme for the development of a nuclear weapon, was "Enormous", an indication of how important the Soviet Union viewed its penetration and the acquisition of its secrets. The GRU's telegram of August 1943 shows that it was already cultivating Dr Allan Nunn May, a brilliant British physicist who had become a secret communist and passed back information on the progress of the atomic bomb project. The KGB's net also encompassed Theodore Hall, who was, however, never prosecuted and, more importantly, Klaus Fuchs (referred to as "F" and "K"in the Soviet files), a German-born British physicist who handed over sketches and details of the specification of the plutonium bomb that was then in the final stages of development.

The Soviet handlers did not neglect their spycraft and in the account of the meeting with Fuchs, great pains are made in detailing the protocol (the agent is to be recognized by having a yellow pencil between two blue ones in his lapel). In their efforts to recruit agents to spy on the OSS, the CIA's Second World War predecessor, Soviet agents were equally fastidious. In a meeting in late September 1945 at Regent's Park Tube Station in London, an agent "Dan" was to be carrying a copy of *John Bull* magazine and before getting down to the serious business of explaining how the OSS operation in London was being wound up, he had to explain to his Soviet handler why he had forgotten to bring along the magazine.

THE VASSILIEV NOTEBOOKS

From Yellow Notebook #1

GRU telegram instructing spying on "Enormous" – code-word for the Manhattan Project, 1943
Report to Merkulov.

1. The material received from our agents shows that work on the investigation of a new, extremely powerful energy source – 'Enormous' – is being conducted at a very intensive pace in the USA and England, and is growing ever larger in scale.

   This problem has received a great deal of attention, it has been allotted extensive scientific and material support and is being worked on by a large contingent of leading physicists.

   As a result even now, despite war-time conditions, exceedingly interesting and important results have been achieved, especially in the USA.

   This problem has major national economic significance, and the application of these works' results will be most significant primarily in the post-war period. A specific issue is the application and use of the results for military technology, namely for the manufacture of uranium bombs...

   The special laboratory at the Academy of Sciences, established at our request by a GKO resolution for the purposes of

expediting our leading scientists' work on 'Enormous' and real-
izing the results of the works of English and Amer. scientists
through the use of agent materials we have obtained, is still in its
organizational stage. The organizational pace is entirely unsatisfactory and the project is taking a very long time to get going.

2. Despite certain achievements by a section of the intelligence operation in obtaining information on the work being done in England
and the USA on 'Enormous', the state of agent cultivation of this
problem and its outlook continues to be unsatisfactory, especially
in the USA. As you know, both we and the GRU NKO are working simultaneously on the agent cultivation of this problem, even
though it is not exclusively a problem of defense and, on the whole,
has broad scientific, technical and applied implications, and is undoubtedly one of the most important projects of our age and a
major achievement for science. The only issue pertaining directly
to military technology is the practical application of this project's
results toward creating atomic super-bomb. By simultaneously cultivating the same narrow, and at the same time authoritative, circle of
scientists and specialists as the GRU, we are essentially doubling our
work. This creates unhealthy competition at work; the same people
are cultivated and recruited (May, Henry Norman – in London;
Oppenheimer – in San Francisco and other), which leads to useless
expenditure of time and energy, and could inevitably lead to the
exposure of our intentions, plans and intelligence activities, and ultimately even to exposures. Therefore, I think it would be expedient
to consolidate efforts to cultivate this problem in the 1st Directorate
of the NKGB USSR and to give it all available GRU agents."

Chief, 1st Dir. of the NKGB USSR
Commissar of State Security, 3rd Rank, Fitin.
11 August 1943

Meeting with Theodore Hall (US atom spy), December 1944

After studying him as much as one could in an hour or an hour and
a half, and getting the impression that he is indeed an intelligent
physicist who used to be in the progressive movement and, while
there, had suffered from the same shortcomings that my son had at

one time suffered from and that were so familiar to me; that he had chosen a very naive means of approach to me (it would have been easier to come to me directly, especially if he had been sent), I instinctually sensed that we could get down to business, especially since I would be the only one at risk if there is an exposure. I thought it would be awkward to end the conversation with nothing or with small-talk, and then bring our man to a meeting with him.

So I said straight out: what's the matter? Let's hear it!

He told me that the new secret weapon was an 'atomic bomb' of colossal destructive capacity.

I interrupted him: Do you understand what you are doing? What makes you think you should reveal the USA's secrets for the USSR's sake? He replied: The S.U. is the only country that could be trusted with such a terrible thing. But since we cannot take it away from other countries – the USSR ought to be aware of its existence and stay abreast of the progress of experiments and construction. This way, at a peace conference, the USSR—on which the fate of my generation depends—will not find itself in the position of a power subjected to blackmail. Don't forget that England is also involved in this secret, completely involved, to the extent that a portion of the experiments and calculations are done in England, and a portion in Canada. All the most outstanding physicists from the USA, England, Italy, Germany (emigrants), and Denmark are working on this thing. The list of physicists is on the last page of his report. We are aware that both Germany and the USSR are working on a shell that operates on the principle of splitting the atom of certain elements (Uranium and anoth. element, which we call Plutonium, and which is the 94th element); however there is little doubt that the USA is ahead of everyone else, because all the best minds from Europe are concentrated here, except for the Russians, and several billions of dollars have been spent on it. Moreover, we have four (or more) cyclotrons, and in other countries there are no more than two in any given country – according to our information. Then, H. started explaining to me in detail the principle on which the bomb operates, as well as the general principle of how the shell is structured, as a kind of cannon within a bomb. Having gone into all the details, he took out a neatly written report and said: There is no way you could have remembered all that, so I prepared you a note. Show this to any physicist, and he will understand what it's about. As for the structure of the shell, it isn't my division, but if necessary, I could find out in detail how it's structured. For now, I know the general structuring principle. The bomb must be dropped from an airplane. According to our calculations, a bomb weighing two tons will have an explosive force equivalent to 20-50 bombs of the same weight. The temperature at detonation will exceed the temp. of the sun's core.

Now I was faced with a dilemma – should I take the report or not? I decided to take it for the following reason: He told me that he had hoped to see at my place a "third person." Now, if he had set up a 'raid' to catch our man red-handed and so forth, there would have been no advantage to handing over the report, and he should have held on to it until a more convenient opportunity. There was an additional reason that supported driving the matter home: There was still the risk that the raid would take place several minutes after he had left, i.e., while the document was in my home. My wife went 'out shopping' and carefully looked the area over, and she did not find anything suspicious.

During the conversation (in reply to my questions), I learned the following, which is not in the report. He works at a center called "Experimental Center Y" (the letter Y) located 35 miles from Santa Fe, New Mexico. This is where work is being done on the shell itself. The center is under the direct authority of the War Department. There are two other centers in the USA – "X" in Tennessee, and "W" in Washington state. There, they are working on preparing the "product," i.e. uranium-235 (at least I think so; I am writing from memory because my wife immediately removed H's report from my house while I went outside and wandered about to lure away any surveillance if there was any). Center "Y" is cordoned off from the outside world by wires and guards and outposts. The workers live within the confines of the fence. Mail is strictly censored. Only recently have they permitted trips further than 75 miles from the center, but for this one needs special permission from the military authorities. He had been allowed to go to NY on leave to see his family. He can go to Santa Fe freely. He proposed that if necessary, he could arrange the meetings so as to report on the progress of experiments, because that is what he thinks is most important, i.e., the most important thing is not the principle itself, which everyone knows, but the status of practical experiments on generating the explosion itself and on controlling the explosion, on the design of the shell, etc. We parted ways having agreed that I would call him in a day or two. He is leaving on Friday at 4 o'clock in the afternoon.

Description and distinguishing features: rather tall, thin, with light brown hair, a pale and slightly pimply face, carelessly dressed; you can tell his boots haven't been cleaned in a long time; his socks are bunched up around the ankles. He wears his hair parted, and it often falls over his forehead. His English is very refined and 'rich'. He answers questions quickly and without the slightest hesitation, especially scientific questions. His eyes are close together.

Obviously – neurasthenic. He is witty and somewhat sarcastic, possibly as a result of premature mental development, but without shades of over-familiarity or cynicism. His chief trait – highly sensitive brain and quick comprehension. In conversation he is as sharp and agile as a rapier.

Addendum: I asked him (half-joking) why he wasn't afraid that I would betray him. He replied: You are known to almost half a million readers and to everyone in the progressive movement. If you can't be trusted, no one can."

Ovakimyan's resol.: Aleksey – what a piece of work! 14.2.45.

Handover notes from KGB in UK to their US colleagues and first meeting with Klaus Fuchs there.

C – NY 26.1.44.

It is proposed to use "Goose" as a contact for "Rest."

Goose's report on a meeting with Rest on Saturday, 5.02.44.

"We were both at the appointed place on time at 4:00 P.M.: he had the green book and the tennis ball and I had the four gloves. I greeted him and he accepted my offer of a walk. We strolled a while and talked.

He is about 5 ft, 10 in., thin, pale complexioned, and at first was very reserved in manner; this last is good. K. dresses well (tweeds) but not fancily. After a ride on the subway, we took a taxi and went to eat. As I kept talking about myself, he warmed up and began to show evidence of getting down to business. For instance, I would say that I had felt honored at having been told to meet him and he said that he "could hardly believe it" when he had been told that we would like him to work with us (this was in England, of course).

The following developed about K.: He obviously has worked with our people before and he is fully aware of what he is doing. Also, he is apparently one of us in spirit. K. has only been here since September but he expects to be here for at least the duration; he may be transferred out of New York, but it is not very likely – in any case he will be able to let us know in plenty of time. He is a mathematical physicist and a graduate of the Universities of Bristol and Edinburgh; he is most likely a very brilliant man to have such a position at his age (he looks about 30).

We took a long walk after dinner and he explained the "factory" set-up: He is a member of a British mission to the U.S. working under the direct control of the U.S. Army; General Somervell and Secretary Stimson are the American heads and Llewellyn was formerly the British representative – Ben Smith, a Laborite, was supposed to take his place but never did, probably on account of his sympathies.

The work resolves itself mainly into a separation of the isotopes of "factory" and is being done thusly: The electronic method has been developed at Berkeley, California and is being carried out practically at a place known only as "Camp Y" - K. believes it is in New Mexico. Working at Berkeley are the Americans Lawrence and Chadwick and the British scientist Oliphant.

Simultaneously, the diffusion method is being tried here in the East; the Englishman Peierls and K. are doing the work in direct co-operation with the Kellogg Co. and the Carbide and Carbon Company. Should the diffusion method prove successful it will be used as a preliminary step in the separation with the final work being done by the electronic method. It is hoped to have the electronic method ready early in 1945 and the diffusion method in July 1945 – but K. says the latter estimate is optimistic. All production will be done in the U.S.; only preparatory work is being carried on in England. K. says that the work is being done in "water-tight compartments" but that he will furnish us with everything in his and Peierls divisions and as much of the other as possible; Peierls is K.'s superior but they have divided the work between them.

The two countries had worked together before 1940 and then there was a lapse till 1942 – even now K. says there is much being withheld from the British. Even Niels Bohr, who is now in this country incognito as Nicholas Baker, has not been told everything.

We made careful arrangements for meeting the next time in two weeks when K. will have information for us.

Note: "Factory" – term for Enormous adopted by G. and R.

Report of visit to Klaus Fuchs

Visit to Klaus 21.02.45. Wednesday.

"Two trips to Boston were necessary in order to see Klaus. The first time I went there on Monday, February 19, I proceeded directly to his sister's home where K. was staying; I did so without a previous telephone call on the possibility that the phone might be watched. When I rang the doorbell (this was at the usual time of 10.15 in the morning) I could see K. inside in the parlor but his sister came to the phone instead and said "K. wants to see you but today is my husband's day off and he is home – also K. is expecting someone from the British Consulate in New York. Please come back Wednesday, if possible".

I said that I would (this only took a few seconds) and walked around Cambridge to think it over; my original intention was to stay over till Tuesday anyhow, but Wednesday made it difficult. So in about an hour I called but when a man's voice that I did not recognize answered, I asked was it a number differing in the last digit from K's and said "sorry" and hung up; this must have been the sister's husband.

There was nothing to do but take the train for home and return on Wednesday and these things I did.

This time the trip was a complete success. I arrived again at the sister's home at exactly the same time in the morning and K. welcomed me most warmly. After distributing the gifts I had for the children and K's sister – as well as the opera wallet for K. – we went back into Boston while K. bought some small items for his friends in Santa Fe, and of course we talked while he explained the situation to me.

It is this:

1. He was not granted a leave at christmas and so was unable to come to Boston till now. The travelling time took away six days so that all he was really left was just a day over a week. K. was due to leave Thursday night.

2. Since he is supposed to make a written report on all people he meets (and in fact even on those at work who speak of the project outside of the actual working hours and outside of their

own particular field), he did not want his brother-in-law to meet me – particularly since the man from the Brit. Consulate was supposed to visit K. either Monday or Tuesday. But for some reason, which K. does not know, this man did not come – which is probably just as well.

3. K. said that he had made a very careful check and was certain that he was not being watched. We returned to Cambridge about 1 o'clock and had a very fine lunch with K's sister. Then we went upstairs and K. outlined the set-up at the camp to me:

    a) When he went there in August there were only 2500 to 3000 people. Now it has expanded to 45000!

    b) The work being carried on is the actual manufacture of "factory" bombs. Employed there are physicists, mathematicians, chemists, engineers: civil, mechanical, electrical, chemical, and many other types of technical help as well as a U.S. Army Engineer Detachment.

    c) They are progressing very well and are expected to go into full scale production in about three months – but K was hesitant about this date and said he would not like to be held to it.

    d) The area is about 40 miles N.W. from Santa Fe and covers the grounds of Los Alamos Ranch, a former Ranch School. R. is allowed only one day a month off to go shopping in Santa Fe (as are all others) and we made a date for the first Saturday in Santa Fe. I am to get off the bus station at Shelby and San Francisco and set my watch by the large clock on San Francisco. Then I am to meet him at 4 PM on the Castillo St. Bridge crossing Santa Fe River. The waiting time is 10 minutes. If we do not meet, the same procedure is to be repeated month after month. Should a substitute have to come (though he would very much prefer me) he is to be identified as follows: the man will have a yellow pencil between two blue ones in his lapel and he will be carrying a copy of Bennett Cerf's Try and Stop Me. K will say to him "How is your brother Raymond?" and the answer will be "Not well, he has been in the hospital for two weeks". The final identification is to be by means of two sections of paper torn in a jagged pattern, one of which K has. K was really prepared and gave me a bus schedule and a map of Santa Fe — he advises me not to go directly there but to a nearby city such as Albuquerque. He also gave me the material which I submitted and we parted at 3:30 PM. My attempt to give him money was unsuccessful — but I did not offend him as I led up to the subject very delicately. He says that he is making all he needs. K does, however, want one thing: when we enter Kiel and Berlin in Germany he wants the Gestapo Headquarters there searched and his dossier (which is very complete) destroyed before it should fall into other hands. This, I told him, we would try to do if at all possible".

"Aleksey's" report on a meeting with Arno 8.03.45.

From Yellow Notebook #2

Account of meeting with contact in London to discuss American OSS

"Vadim" — to C 6.8.45 "Stan" ("Dan") got a job in the Russian division of the OSS. He was assigned to work in London and will work on questions pertaining to the USSR. His assignments from the OSS: 1. Shedding light on the activities of Arcos and Amtorg; 2. Soviet transport, checking and comparing railroad network maps in American and British possession; 3. The question of the military potential of the Trans-Siberian RR, 4. Information on the Baikal-Amur mainline; 5. the exact location, main technical personnel, output, transition to new types of production, working conditions, and application of new industrial procedures at machine building factories in the USSR; 6. information on metallurgy, rubber, and chemical industries; data on war casualties; data on public health; age distribution of the R.A., and the distribution and composition of R.A. units in the Far East; reports on Soviet policies toward countries that were liberated from the enemy and former satellites; information about Vlasov's movement, his whereabouts, his fate and the fate of his supporters, and the reasons for his going over to Hitler; the uses of mountain mineshaft equipment being imported into the USSR. "While looking through 'Cabin's' files on Soviet railway transport, 'Stan' found a detailed report on the Baikal-Amur mainline, dated October 1943, and issued by the commander of the Amur naval flotilla, Junior

Captain Brakhtman. It is impossible to determine how the report got there, but judging from its contents, Captain Brakhtman had been used unwittingly. In the same file, 'Stan' saw a photo of a tunnel under the Amur river that was taken by a certain Major Nelson, who had supposedly been assigned to the R.A. as an expert on tanks." + Stan gave a description of the work of the Russian division of "Cabin," along with descriptions of the people working there.

"Vadim" – to C 4.9.45 In the middle of August, Dan left for London. He and "Raid" agreed on secret meeting conditions. Every Sunday, beginning on September 2nd, D. will arrive for the meeting at 20.00 and wait 10–15 min. by the exit of the metro station "Regent Park." He will be holding the magazine "John Bull." Our man: "Didn't I meet you at Vick's restaurant at Connecticut Avenue?" – "Yes, Vick himself introduced you." Afterwards, the operational officer should produce the price tag that was sent to C., and Dan should show his exact duplicate. + a photo of "Dan" was sent to C. "Pancake" – the well-known Amer. journalist Isidor Stone.

Report on the meeting with "Dan" on 23.09.45 Operative "Alan" (known to Dan as "Mike")

When I arrived at the agreed-upon time at the exit of the 'Regents Park' Tube station, I noticed an American officer in uniform standing by the exit who looked the same age as 'Dan'; however, he did not have the aforementioned magazine 'John Bull'. Walking past him as the clock struck 8, I also noticed that the officer looked at his watch. When I got to the corner, I turned back and walked down the opposite side of the street. Meanwhile, the officer had taken from his pocket some kind of book or magazine. I crossed the street and walked up to the Tube station. It turned out that he was holding some kind of book. It was seven minutes past eight, and there was nothing left for me to do but to try to talk to this officer. I started my conversation as follows:

　　Me: Do you have a light? Him: Yes, please. Me: Thank you… Women, they're never on time, are they … I take it you're also waiting for your girlfriend? Him: No, I'm waiting for a friend. Me: Been out of the States long? Him: No, not too long… Me: I've been to the

USA, too. It made quite an impression on me. Him: Were you there a long time ago? Me: Oh, it was relatively long ago, in 1939. Him: Where did you go when you were there? Me: NY. It's quite different from London. I liked NY, with its big buildings and restaurants. It's a lively, cheerful city. I spent a lot of time in restaurants there. I especially liked this one restaurant there called "Vick's." Him: The one on Connecticut Avenue. Me: Oh yes. Come to think of it, you look sort of familiar. Didn't we meet there? Him: That's right—Vick himself introduced us. When he had spoken his password, I became confident that he was indeed "Dan." We shook hands and continued talking, and "Dan" invited me to go back to his apartment.

Just then, a policeman walked by us, and so for the sake of appearances, I gladly took him up on his offer. When we had gone a bit further from the station, D. said that I had given him the password incorrectly. I explained to him why this had happened and repeated my password as it was stipulated, adding that I had a small card for him. (The cards were identical. They are enclosed). When I said that I had expected him to be holding "John Bull," and that this was the only sign I had to go by, "Dan" replied that he had already gone to the meeting place three times with "John Bull," but had practically lost hope of contacting us, become upset, and forgotten it today. He wanted to know why it had taken us so long to show up for the meeting. With regard to the sign, he was sure that we ought to have a photo of him, because he had provided two of his cards expressly for that purpose before leaving. During the conversation, "Dan" remarked that, in essence, he had agreed to come here in order to help us here. "If I hadn't met up with you, there wouldn't have been any point in coming here at all," he said. The source described the situation in his agency. Because the agency is being transferred to the State Dep., it is possible that he will have to return home in October. This isn't certain though. Maybe he will stay here.

Report on the meeting of 24.09.45

The source reported that in connection with the liquidation of the official branch of the OSS in London and the subordination of the entire OSS in the country, there had been some changes. Today he learned with absolute certainty that he would be receiving an order reassigning him to the country. Personally, he thinks that his departure will be much more useful than if he were to stay here. He explains this by the fact that he will arrive in the county just as the personnel is being reorganized. As for the reasons for the liquidation of the OSS branch in London, Dan says that it has to do with the complication of the relationship between the island and the country. If in the past they had collaborated on all their work on the East, and the island had occasionally allowed the country to make use of its secret information, now the island refused to collaborate or allow its information to be used. The work of the London branch of the OSS will be conducted via official government agencies on the island. Regarding the nature of the materials he had brought, D. said the following: "On the whole, it's all straightforward. Some of the reports I had to recall from memory, as it has been a long time since the material passed through my hands. The only thing that might be unclear to you is the matter with the Soviet prisoners of war. But I'm not even sure if this is of interest to you." D. then gave me a detailed account of how, on the continent, they used our prisoners of war to obtain information about the Soviet Union. The report is enclosed. In light of his planned departure, I asked about arranging to meet with him in the country. To this, D replied that it was unnecessary, because the comrade who had connected us was a personal friend of his, and he would have no trouble renewing contact with him.

We agreed to meet again the following Saturday, September 29th, in front of the exit of the "Swiss Cottage" Tube station on the Bakerloo Line, at 3 o'clock in the afternoon. Because yesterday, as he was leaving, D. had said, offhandedly: "I'll get on this bus and it will take me straight home," I noted that he did not completely check out. Today I pointed out this flaw to him, to which he replied that he did not have any experience in these matters. In the country, he would meet with his friend, with whom he could show up anywhere. D asked me to explain how this was done. I briefly explained it to him, taking the local surroundings into consideration. D reported orally that they use two code words to refer to the "Intelligence Service" (British) "Broadway," and occasionally "Coal" (Coal). This is frequently used in telephone conversations.

Penkovsky's Operational Plan

Unlike the wealth of information concerning Cold War activities which emerged from the KGB archives during the early 1990s, Western intelligence services such as MI6 and the CIA have allowed relatively little post-Second World War material to be released. One of the few exceptions is the operational plan for the handling of dead drops for the GRU defector Oleg Penkovsky in Moscow, who leaked around 10,000 pages of documents to the United States and United Kingdom. The dead drop plan was especially vital, as direct physical contact with agents in the Soviet Union was perilous and rarely attempted; Penkovsky's contact in the US embassy, the agricultural attaché, only succeeded in this once, when a package was handed over in the toilets of the US ambassador's residence.

The dead drops were designed with meticulous precision; Penkovsky himself needed to be briefed on their location and the protocol of leaving and retrieving documents while on a visit to Helsinki, where he was less exposed to surveillance. The research needed to identify and vet the dead drop site was extremely thorough, including ensuring that the site (a phone booth) was not overlooked by too many windows and that the lobby of the apartment building where it was located could be entered by a Westerner without suspicion. The container in which the documents at the dead drop were to be loaded also had to have its paint matched precisely to the shade of green of the phone booth's radiator, not an easy task for a US intelligence operative in 1960s' Moscow!

In the event, most of Penkovsky's contacts were with Janet Chisholm, the wife of his main MI6 contact, who used a "brush contact" technique in which packages were exchanged as the two of them moved close together as they walked, often shielded by Chisholm's children. It was during one such exchange that they were spotted by a KGB surveillance team. It took a little while for Soviet intelligence to identify him, but after this he was arrested and the KGB arranged for the signal for the unloading of the telephone booth dead drop to be transmitted (a silent call with breathing followed by a mark on a telegraph pole). When Penkovsky's American liaison turned up to the dead drop site he was apprehended by four KGB officers, and the defector's fate was sealed.

•••••••• OPERATIONAL PLAN

I. CASING OF DROP SITE

It is proposed that we brief •••••••• immediately, instructing him to case this area thoroughly. It is envisioned that •••••••• should first stroll past the drop site for external observations, and later, at an interval of several days, enter the site area and place a telephone call to a pre-arranged contact or absenteed Embassy acquaintance—whose absence has been previously ascertained. (See Annex I for detailed casing brief for •••••••• guidance.)

II. CASING OF SIGNAL SITE

After a thorough casing and examination of the proposed dead drop site, •••••••• should case the signal site proposed by •••••••• This casing can be done simultaneously with the casing of the dead drop site since it is believed that it is unnecessary to physically enter the signal site proper. In fact, the undersigned urges that •••••••• not enter the signal site area (to use the phone) for security reasons. A passing, external inspection should be sufficient. (See Annex III for signal site brief for •••••••• guidance.)

III. INTERNAL COMMUNICATION WITH ••••••••

A.   Loading Pre-selected Drop
1. Upon receipt of •••••••• detailed casing information regarding site characteristics and •••••••• determination of •••••••• date of arrival in Helsinki, it is proposed that CSR/9 and/or the undersigned (or CSR/9's designee(s)) proceed to Helsinki for the purpose of briefing and further training •••••••• to put down the pre-selected drop. The actual drop will consist of acknowledgement of •••••••• first communication and a detailed plan designed to enable •••••••• to deposit additional materials in a drop selected and affording maximal control by CIA. (See outgoing communications from ••••••••)
2. The drop packet and contents will be prepared at Headquarters and should be hermetically sealed (to deter opening by •••••••• as well as to protect the contents) and colored to match the dark green radiator drop site. GSR/9 will hand-carry the packet to Helsinki for transmittal to ••••••••

3. In Helsinki, •••••••• will be given intensive briefing on the general and specific locale, avenue(s) of approach, loading, security factors, aborting measures, possible entrapment including KGB M. O. against •••••••• if apprehended, use of telephone to call wife, exiting direction, and signalling technique and procedure. To give realism to the briefing, a building with foyer area, similar to the actual drop site, will attempted to be found in the Helsinki area and actual practice(s) will be performed.

4. •••••••• will then be given the packet to secrete upon himself as he returns to Moscow. (Note: •••••••• has a diplomatic passport and has previously reported that he has never been searched or asked to declare his personal items to Customs.) Upon arrival in Moscow, •••••••• will transfer the packet to his maximum security safe to which he alone has the key and combination. The safe is located in a secure building. (If preferred, the packet could be retained upon his body until, the drop is effected.)

5. As soon as possible, •••••••• will make a dry run <u>up</u> Pushkinskaya Ulitsa for the purpose of external casing and orientation of the building drop site. At an interval of several days, he will make the actual drop preferably just before dusk, late in the day. It is suggested that consideration be given to •••••••• proceeding along Kuznetskiy Most, turning abruptly right onto Pushkinskaya Ulitsa, and, at his normal (fast) pace, proceeding directly into the drop site locale and emplacing the drop. An alternative method might be to proceed down Kuznetskiy Most and observe the window "displays" in Meat Store No. 19, turning onto Pushkinskaya Ulitsa, (still window shopping in the Meat Store), pause and then proceed into the building site and place a call to his wife inquiring as to what kind of meat or <u>kolbasa</u> his wife prefers him to purchase. This would give him a convincing cover for the use of the phone, although his surveillants might be closer because he slowed down to window shop.

6. If, for any reason, •••••••• is obliged to abort the actual loading of the drop, then he should make, at this time, <u>only one more</u> attempt at an interval of approximately one week. If a second attempt must be made, •••••••• should use the alternate plan for approach and not the exact one as before.

7. After successful loading of the drop, •••••••• should allow at least
    one day to pass, but not more than two, before he puts down
    the pre-selected signal at the pre-designated site. On the basis of
    •••••••• casing report, •••••••• can proceed to this site and mark
    the loading signal with a red crayon or pen.

IV. OUTGOING COMMUNICATION FROM ••••••••

A. It is proposed that in our message to •••••••• that we inform him
    of the following method in which he may communicate with us:

1. •••••••• will be instructed that the American House, No. 3
    KROPOTKINSKAYA NABERZHNAYA, will be the locale
    for the drop. He will be instructed to proceed down the right
    side of TURCHANIN Ulitsa (toward the Moscow River) at a
    specified date and time, and as he passes the wall surrounding
    the American House courtyard, throw the drop package over
    the wall. •••••••• will be in place on the otherside of the wall to
    retrieve the package. (See attached diagram and 1955 photos of
    this area – Annex IV.)
2. Upon receipt of package •••••••• will secrete it upon himself and
    return immediately to the Embassy for inclusion of package in
    pouch. NOTE: Dependent upon the circumstances and ••••••••
    recommendations, it may be more propitious to use the Marine
    NCO (highly recommended by •••••••• for actual transport of
    the drop packet to the Embassy. Thus, •••••••• could leave emp-
    ty-handed and upon safe-arrival at the Embassy could telephone
    •••••••• at the American House. This would be the signal for
    •••••••• to instruct the Marine NCO to leave for the Embassy.
    However, such action might not be amenable to •••••••• without
    Ambassadorial knowledge and concurrence.
3. The afore-mentioned plan is contingent upon •••••••• casing of
    the area and his recommendations for implementing the plan. (A
    briefing guide is attached as Annex V for •••••••• guidance.)

ANNEX I

1. As soon as possible, •••••••• should take a stroll up the right-hand
    side of PUSHKINSKAYA Ulitsa (going toward SADOVAYA)

and closely observe Building No. 2, situated between the Women's Shoe Store and Meat Store No. 19, located near the intersection of PUSHKINSKAYA Ulitsa and KUZNETSKIY MOST. (See Attachment No. 1 – map of area.)

2. During •••••••• walk-by and visual inspection of Building No. 2 and the immediate vicinity, the following detailed information is desired:

    a. What type of building does No. 2 appear to be? Apartment-house, shop, restaurant, warehouse, etc.?

    b. Would a Westerner be able to enter the ground floor to use the telephone without arousing undue attention?

    c. Is the telephone booth visible when walking past the building?

    d. Are there any windows flanking the entrance which would enable passersby to look into the lobby or foyer on the ground floor?

    e. Was the presence of any type of possible fixed security forces noted in the immediate vicinity?

    f. Note surveillance patterns on •••••••• in this area and the closeness of •••••••• surveillants, if possible (without arousing their suspicions).

    g. Did •••••••• note any people transiting (entering or departing) or loitering in the lobby/foyer of Building No. 2 as •••••••• passed?

    h. What type of building is located directly across the street from Building No. 2 with respect to its adaptability as an observation post?

NOTE: To facilitate •••••••• ability to observe the numerous items enumerated above, it is suggested that •••••••• pause at several stores along PUSHKINSKAYA Ulitsa to "window shop." In fact, •••••••• might window shop at the [illegible hand annotation] on the corner of PUSHKINSKAYA Ulitsa and KUZNETSKIY MOST (note location on attached map) and even enter and purchase a book. Upon exiting •••••••• could cross the street and window shop in Meat Store No. 19. With regard to the meat store, CIA would be interested in knowing if there is an entrance on KUZNETSKIY MOST as well as on PUSHKINSKAYA Ulitsa. Also what are the operating hours of the meat shop?

3. At an interval of several days, preferably at dusk, •••••••• should walk toward PUSHKINSKAYA Ulitsa past the PROEZD KHU-DOZHESTVENNOGO TEATRA, turn right onto PUSHKIN-SKAYA Ulitsa and enter Building No. 2 and place a telephone call (telephone No. 28) to a friend in the Embassy. (This call should be pre-arranged to •••••••• or so arranged that •••••••• will know that the recipient of the call is not present to answer the call.) The location of the telephone is contained in the attached map and is situated to the left of the entrance.

4. The following detailed information is desired in conjunction with this casing/observation plan:

    a. <u>Surveillance</u>: Number and pattern. Did any follow •••••••• into Building No. 2? <u>Is it possible to enter Building No. 2 before the surveillance turns the corner?</u>

    b. Sketch and describe interior of foyer or lobby.

        (1) Are there apt to be people loitering inside?
        (2) Where are the stairs located?
        (3) What color are the walls? Type of floor?
        (4) What type of lighting is used in the lobby? How bright?
        (5) Is phone booth illuminated?
        (6) Note any other entrances or exits.

    c. Particularly note dark green radiator near wall, opposite telephone booth, and to right of the entrance.

        (1) Match green color as close as possible with colors from your chart. Is finish flat or shiny? New or old? Is it smooth or cracked and peeling.
        (2) If •••••••• can determine a standard green available in Moscow, and visual observation confirms that this is the same shade of green as the radiator, he may possibly be able to duplicate it from Embassy stocks.
        (3) It may be that the paint inside other Moscow building entrances is similar in color to that of the radiator site.

Therefore, •••••••• may be able to get a sample, away from the site, after he has observed the radiator coloring.

(4) How high is radiator off of floor? Length?

(5) Note peculiar or distinguishing characteristics.

(6) What is the approximate distance between wall and back of radiator?

(7) What are the lighting conditions here?

(8) Is the hook visible? What color is the hook?

(9) Would a small packet, the color of the radiator, be visible to people entering or loitering in the foyer/lobby?

(10) Are there knobs or dials for manual operation of the radiator?

(11) When will central heat be turned on in Moscow?

NOTE: In order to observe radiator area closely, •••••••• might, if he deems it secure, loiter just briefly near the radiator before exiting. •••••••• could be buttoning his coat, lighting a cigarette, blowing nose, etc.)

ANNEX II

The utilization of •••••••• in the project •••••••• presupposes that a risk assessment has been resolved in favor of using •••••••• instead of an unprotected American tourist. The involvement of •••••••• also is predicated on the fact that because of the prohibition on the use of American Embassy personnel, no active support can be rendered by CIA staff agents attached to the American Embassy, Moscow. The decision to use the services of •••••••• was based on the above premises plus the fact that •••••••• has diplomatic immunity, that he is trained in operational support tasks, capable, well motivated, and has already established operational patterns. Moreover, in case of a provocation, no American would be involved directly. On the debit side of the ledger, it should be noted that •••••••• is not CIA controlled (joint liaison operation), that he will probably render a full report of his operational involvement to his superiors, that ••• will become involved in this operation, and that •••••••• must be met in Helsinki in order to rehearse all steps of the plan and to give Subject the drop instrument.

ANNEX III

SIGNAL SITE CASING

1. Approach from Ulitsa GORKOGO going toward Ulitsa PUSH-KINSKAYA via KOZITSKIY Pereulok. Walk on right side of street. Window-shop in vegetable-fruit store which is next to site (House 2, Korpus 8).
2. Determine type of installation where telephone is located.
3. Is telephone (and signal site) visible from sidewalk? Are there windows on ground floor level?
4. Would a Westerner have normal access in terms of using telephone or is telephone so hidden that passersby would never be aware of its existence? Are there any written signs or overt indications that there is a telephone booth in this location?
5. Observe any taxi stands or possible fixed surveillance/observation points near this building.
6. Notice if any people are loitering near entrance to building or situated across the street.
7. If you can observe interior through window or open door as you pass by, describe in detail interior arrangements.
8. Observe type of building(s) opposite (across the street) from signal site.

[*Missing Text*]

4. The advantages of this type of outgoing communication from •••••••• is that, if this operation is being mounted by the KGB as a provocation, it puts the opposition in an extremely difficult position in terms of making a positive identification of •••••••• and of physically apprehending him. Thus it affords CIA stricter control of the drop and area than heretofore has been possible for internal drop unloading.
5. It is proposed that •••••••• be informed that "our" man" will be available, i.e., waiting on the other side of the wall, precisely at 2300 hours (e. g.) on each Saturday for four concurrent weeks. "Our man" will be instructed to be in place at 2255 and remain in place until circa 2305. In the event that something is amiss, "our man" will give a danger signal, e. g., sing or whistle a familiar tune. Moreover,

a precise spot along the wall will be located for •••••••• to throw the packet.

6.   •••••••• will have the option of aborting the proposed action as he passes the drop spot. If the operation is clean, •••••••• only security worry will be the presence and/or location of Soviet citizens in the immediate area. However, in the past, this street has been dimly lit and not subject to heavy pedestrian traffic.

7.   Exact details and timing will be worked out upon approval of this operational plan by CSR/9 and the casing and recommendations of ••••••••

CHAPTER 4

ACTIVE MEASURES AND SUBVERSION

Protocol 'M'

In addition to cultivating agents well placed to betray the other side's military and economic secrets, Cold War intelligence agencies engaged in vigorous campaigns of disinformation to destabilize the other side and to paint them in the worst possible light in front of states and sectors of society already disinclined to trust them. The KGB had a whole department, Department A, of its First Chief Directorate (which ran operations outside the Soviet Union) dedicated to such *dezinformatsya* ("disinformation"). The CIA and MI6 also attempted such "active measures", but the difficulties of freely moving or contacting agents inside the Soviet bloc tempered their effectiveness.

In the late 1940s, concern was growing that the Soviet success in installing puppet regimes throughout eastern Europe after the end of the Second World War might be repeated by a further communist push westwards into Italy and Germany. In light of this, the publication of Protocol M in a West German newspaper, *Der Kurier*, in January 1948 was particularly worrying. It seemed to be a blueprint compiled by the Cominform (the organization which both united international communist parties and kept them firmly under Soviet domination) to incite a communist revolution in Germany. Using the rallying cry of opposition to the Marshall Plan, the US-brokered injection of aid to revive the war-ravaged economies of Europe, Protocol M envisaged a series of transport strikes to paralyze the German economy, followed by a more general programme of agitation by trades unions, culminating in a general strike and an appeal for Soviet assistance.

In fact, Protocol M was itself most likely a piece of disinformation by the Western allies, designed to highlight the (undoubtedly real) danger of communist subversion by leaking an especially alarming (though faked) example. The British distributed a large number of copies in their zone of occupation in Germany, while in the House of Commons, the Foreign Office Minister Hector McNeil warned that the Protocol "has been compiled from authoritative Communist sources, and this is corroborated by information already in our possession." In a delicious irony, McNeil's own private secretary had been until very recently Guy Burgess, one of the Soviet Union's most successful British agents and a member of the Cambridge Spy Ring with Kim Philby and Donald Maclean. In December 1947, Burgess was posted to the newly formed Information Research Department, established precisely to counter Soviet propaganda, so placing a Soviet spy at the very heart of the British disinformation effort.

PROTOCOL 'M'

The coming winter will see the decisive epoch in the history of the German working class. In conjunction with the entire working class in all European countries it will gain power through an energetic campaign for the key positions in production. This is not a manœuvre for obtaining ministerial appointments but for the starting positions in the final battle for the liberation of the world proletariat. Discipline of the comrades and ruthless activity of every functionary are the prerequisites for the final victory, so soon to come, of the working class. There must not be any doubt that for the sake of this final victory all the paraphernalia of the proletarian battle will be put into operation. The motherland of socialism, the Soviet Union, can and will support the fight against the powers of monopoly-capitalism with all and every means.

The Communist Information Centre (Cominform) will co-ordinate the common fight of all the socialist movements in Europe. Although the German Party is not yet a member of this Centre, the Party holds a key position in the coming campaign. It has to conduct the battle for the European centre of production in the Ruhr area. The entire working class of all nations will furnish the necessary means. The German Party has the task of using these means ruthlessly wherever it can be done to the greatest advantage.

The object of the winter campaign is to repel the monopolistic-capitalistic attack of the so-called Marshall Plan.

After extensive discussions the comrade functionaries have come to the following decisions:

Part 1

The centres of the battle of the masses are:

(i)   The Ruhr area and its production, and
(ii) The means of transport in West and North Germany.

For tactical reasons it is necessary that the comrade functionaries are not in the front line when the strikes break out. But in accordance with Plan R experienced functionaries in the strike cadres are required to ensure, with even more care than hitherto, that the workers' risings occur simultaneously in transport and production. The trade unions of the transport and iron and steel workers will carry out a succession of strikes. The Party must in all circumstances refrain from any operations. It will have to reckon with its prohibition by the military authorities. The plan for the new organization must therefore be carried out with the utmost speed.

From past experience it must be expected that the Ruhr workers will be given substantial preferential treatment, with the result that the strike idea may be rejected for opportunist reasons. In this respect it is up to the transport worker to perform his task. Special importance is to be attached to the railway lines from Bremen to Dusseldorf and from Hamburg to Bielefeld. Key point of the transport workers' strike is Dortmund. Essen must not be permitted to gain preponderance through wild strikes; this would jeopardize the entire plan. It appears from previous communications that the military authorities are already organizing lorry transport which could take over soon after the railways and private lorry transport have come to a standstill. It is there fore necessary to find out the likely routes (earmarked by the military) and to sabotage the supply lines. Foodstuffs should not thereby be destroyed; the aim is only to prevent their punctual arrival. The co-ordination in time of delays in the arrival of food transports and the organization of wild strikes, leading to a loss of production, is an essential feature of the operation. Comrades …(here follow their names) will be at their posts from the middle of November on, as previously announced. Security measures for these posts have been taken by the cadres and the funds for strike pay are available. The leading principle for strikers in other parts of the West remains as hitherto: their aim must be the unity of the working class.

Part 2

As far as organization is concerned, it is based on the iron and steel workers' union. But it must not be neglected to obtain or control if possible the position of treasurer in every union.

Up to now all attempts in this direction have failed. Should it not be possible to win over a sufficient number of agents before the appointed day, it must be ensured that the task can be fulfilled under the leadership of social-democratic comrades. In this event the Party must, by agitation, see to it that the R-men, from below, succeed in getting the time-table adopted, and thereby restrict the liberty of action of the Schumacher people (viz. the Social-democrats). The unity of the working class must at this moment become a reality, even if this involves renunciation of complete control.

The cadres have the special task of ascertaining the weaknesses in the mass organization of the Social-democratic Party. Subsequently they will be ruthlessly exploited.

Internal trade union negotiations must be initiated forthwith. It must be attempted to obtain organizational control of the iron and steel workers' union by yielding other positions.

All appointments have already been made. Comrades...(here follow the names) have been approved as members of the executive committee for Operation Ruhr. They can be reached at any time under the known code names.

Part 3

Agitation will be uniformly directed by the central executive committee. Propaganda targets are:

(i)   The Marshall Plan, as a plan by the monopoly-capitalists in the U.S.A. for enslavement.
(ii) The strikes in countries dominated by the monopoly-capitalists, as an indication of the quickening dissolution of capitalistic society.
(iii) The serene and progressive development of the east-European economy under the protection of the Soviet Union.

Press polemics have principally to concern themselves with the protests by non-Communists against the dismantling in the West. They are an attempt to protect future capitalist markets. Since a complete prohibition of all Party Papers has to be reckoned with, stationary transmitters and the established courier network will continuously provide agitation and information material. It must be ensured that the receiving sets which have been provided are installed in time and safe against sequestration.

It is the task of agitation cadres 7, 11 and 14 to popularize the plebiscite and the socialization of the Ruhr industry. It is necessary to conduct, together with the Social Democrats, a campaign at public meetings on this common basis. The unity of the working class must be promoted by means of this joint propaganda for a plebiscite. It is quite agreeable to the central executive committee that the Social Democrats should, at first, hold the important positions in the joint action committees.

Part 4

Time-table:

(a) Until the end of December: Arranging a common basis between the Social Democrats and the Communist Party for a plebiscite.
(b) Until the end of February: Organization of strike cadres.
(c) From the beginning of March on: Organization of the general strike.

If necessary, the time-table may be changed. The central executive committee is in permanent session and at all times prepared to make amendments or issue directives if required.

Part 5

The MA cadres are entrusted with supervision. Ando 47 105 and 47 109 are applicable. Punctual execution of the cadres' directives by the comrade functionaries must be ensured.

V. I. Lenin: "He who puts first in his programme, tactics and organizational work, the political mass agitation which reaches the entire population, runs the least risk of failure in the revolution."

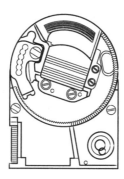

Microdot viewer

Microdots, tiny miniaturized photographs which need a powerful magnifier
to view, were a perfect way of passing secret information. This East German
Uranus-M camera could both produce and view microdots and was small
enough when the viewing tube was removed to be concealed inside a regular 35mm film canister.

Microfiche copier

In the 1970s the KGB produced a specially modified copier, the Zachiyt,
which was able to duplicate microfiche, thereby solving the technical problem associated with the increasing number of classified documents being
held in that format. The Zachiyt was concealed inside a book and could
make 35 copies before it needed recharging.

Soviet Plan to Discredit Dulles

The KGB pursued "active measures" vigorously throughout the early Cold War. As tensions between the USSR and the United States rose to a crescendo in the early 1960s, such operations grew more widespread and daring. These ranged from faked correspondence between Stalin and the Yugoslav leader Tito, designed to expose the alleged Trotsykist leanings of the latter, to a series of attacks on Jewish cemeteries in Germany intended to highlight the continued activities of neo-Nazis in the Allied-occupied zones of the country. The downing of an American U-2 reconnaissance plane over the Soviet Union in May 1960 and the capture alive of its pilot, Gary Powers, presented the Soviets with a propaganda coup at the same time as it dangerously inflamed the tempers of the two sides' intelligence organizations.

The memorandum from Alexander Shelepin, the KGB's second head, to the Committee of State Security of the USSR, which sets out a detailed plan to discredit his arch-rival Allan Dulles, Director of the CIA, refers directly to the U-2 incident as the catalyst for this bold manoeuvre. The KGB sought in particular to exploit rivalry between the CIA and its domestic equivalent, the FBI, to cast doubt on the competence of Dulles and his agency. This included employing the services of the American communist writer Albert Kahn to write a satirical piece lampooning Dulles and writing forged letters, purporting to be from CIA officers, which would criticize his leadership. In the international sphere, the KGB could be more creative, including exposing the links between the CIA and the OUN, the Ukrainian Nationalist movement, which continued a rearguard struggle against Soviet occupation until the early 1950s, and arranging the return to Soviet allegiance of agents who had defected in Germany, who would then hold press conferences denouncing their American former paymasters. The Shelepin plan extended to smear operations against Dulles in Iran, Palestine, Egypt, Japan and Indonesia, as well as using allegations that he accepted bribes from the Lockheed Corporation to rouse congressional indignation against him at home. Little of this, however, ever came to pass and Dulles remained in place until forced to resign following the April 1961 Bay of Pigs incident, a botched CIA-sponsored invasion of Cuba to overthrow Fidel Castro's revolutionary communist government.

SOVIET PLAN TO DISCREDIT DULLES

Note from KGB Chairman A. Shelepin to Central Committee of the Communist Party of the Soviet Union, Regarding Plan to Discredit CIA Chief Dulles

USSR Top Secret

Committee of State Security

Council of Ministers of the USSR 7 June 1960

CC CPSU

The failure of the intelligence action prepared by the Central Intelligence Agency (CIA) with the plane "Lockheed U-2" caused an aggravation of existing tensions between the CIA and other USA intelligence services and the Federal Bureau of Investigation (FBI), and also provoked protests by the American public and certain members of the Congress, who are demanding investigation of the CIA activities.

The Committee of state security considers it advisable to make use of this newly complex situation and to carry out the following measures targeted at further discrediting CIA activity and compromising its leader Allen DULLES:

1. In order to activate a campaign by DULLES' political and personal opponents:

    a) to mail to them anonymous letters using the names of CIA officials criticizing its activity and the authoritarian leadership of DULLES;

    b) to prepare a dossier which will contain publications from the foreign press and declarations of officials who criticized the CIA and DULLES personally, and to send it, using the name of one of the members of the Democratic Party, to the Fulbright Committee [the Senate Committee on Foreign Relations] which is conducting an investigation into CIA activities in relation to the failure of the summit;

    c) to send to some members of Congress, to the Fulbright Committee, and to the FBI specially prepared memos from two or three officials of the State Department with attached private letters, received (allegedly) from now deceased American diplomats, which would demonstrate CIA involvement in domestic decision-making, the persecution of foreign diplomats who took an objective stand, and which also would point out that, for narrow bureaucratic purposes, the CIA puts deliberately false data into information for the State Department;

d) to study the possibility and, if the opportunity presents itself, to prepare and disseminate through appropriate channels a document by former USA Secretary of State F. DULLES, which would make it clear that he exploited the resources of A. DULLES as leader of the CIA to fabricate compromising materials on his private and political adversaries;

e) to prepare, publish and disseminate abroad a satirical pamphlet on A. DULLES, using the American writer Albert KAHN who currently stays in Moscow to write the pamphlet.

2. With the aim of further exposing the activities of American intelligence in the eyes of the public and to create preconditions with which the FBI and other USA intelligence services could substantiate their opinion about the CIA's inability to conduct effective intelligence:

a) to fabricate the failure of an American agent "Fyodorov," dropped in the Soviet Union by plane in 1952 and used by organs of the KGB in an operational game with the adversary.

To publish in the Soviet press an announcement about the arrest of "Fyodorov" as an American agent and, if necessary, to arrange a press-conference about this affair;

b) to agree with Polish friends about the exposure of the operational game led by the organs of the KGB along with the MSS PPR [Ministry of State Security of the Polish People's Republic] with a "conduit" on the payroll of American intelligence of the Organization of Ukrainian Nationalists (OUN) – "Melnikovists." To this end to bring back to Poland the Polish MSS agent "Boleslav," planted in the course of this game on the OUN "conduit," and to arrange for him to speak to the press and radio about subversive activity by American intelligence against the USSR and PPR. To arrange, in addition, for public appearances by six American intelligence agents dropped on USSR and PPR territory as couriers of the "conduit" in the course of the game;

c) to suggest to the security bodies of the GDR that they arrange public trials for the recently arrested agents of American intelligence RAUE, KOLZENBURG, GLAND, USCH-INGER and others.

To arrange for wide coverage of the trials' materials in the media of the GDR and abroad; [text omitted]

3. To utilize, provided our Hungarian friends agree, the American intelligence documents they obtained in the U.S. mission in Budapest to compromise the CIA and to aggravate the differences between the CIA and other intelligence services by publicizing some of the documents or by sending them to the FBI.

If necessary, the necessary documents should be forged using the existing samples.

4. In order to create mistrust in the USA government toward the CIA and to produce an atmosphere of mutual suspicion within the CIA staff, to work out and implement an operation creating the impression of the presence in the CIA system of KGB agents recruited from among rank-and-file American intelligence officers, who, following their recruitment, admit their guilt, allegedly on the order of Soviet intelligence. To stage for this purpose a relevant conversation within range of a [CIA] listening device, as well as the loss of an address book by a Soviet intelligence officer with the telephone number of a CIA official; to convey specially prepared materials to the adversary's attention through channels exposed to him, etc.

5. To work out and implement measures on blowing the cover of several scientific, commercial and other institutions, used by the CIA for its spy activities. In particular, to carry out such measures with regard to the "National Aeronautics and Space

Administration" [NASA] and the "Informational Agency" of the USA [U.S. Information Agency (USIA)].

6. In order to disclose the subversive activities of the CIA against some governments, political parties and public figures in capitalist countries, and to foment mistrust toward Americans in the government circles of these countries, to carry out the following:

a) to stage in Indonesia the loss by American intelligence officer PALMER, who is personally acquainted with President SUKARNO and exerts a negative influence on him, a briefcase containing documents jointly prepared by the MFA [Ministry of Foreign Affairs] of the USSR which apparently belong to the CIA station in Jakarta and which provide evidence of USA plans to utilize American agents and rebel forces to overthrow the government of SUKARNO;

b) to carry out measures, with regard to the arrest in February of this year in the UAR [United Arab Republic] of a group of Israeli intelligence agents, to persuade the public in the UAR and Arab countries that American intelligence is linked to the activities of those agents and coordinates its work in the Arab East with Israeli intelligence.

To compromise, to this end, American intelligence officers KEMP and CONNOLLY who work under cover of the UN commission observing the armistice in Palestine;

c) to prepare and implement measures to make public the fact that American intelligence made use of the Iranian newspapers "Fahrman" and "Etelliat," specifically mentioning the names of their agents (Abbas SHAHENDEH, Jalal NEMATOLLAKHI); [text omitted]

7. To work out measures which, upon implementation, would demonstrate the failure of the CIA efforts to actively on a concrete factual basis use various émigré centers for subversive work against countries in the socialist camp.

In particular, using the example of the anti-Soviet organization "The Union of the Struggle for the Liberation of the Peoples of Russia" (SBONR), to discredit in the eyes of American taxpayers the activities of American intelligence in funding émigré organizations. To bring to light, along with other measures, real or forged American intelligence documents on its finances and guidance of subversive activities of the SBONR.

8. With the means available of the KGB to promote inquiries in the parliaments of England, France and other countries of their governments about their attitude to the hostile actions of USA intelligence intended to aggravate international tension.

9. To arrange public appearances by distinguished public and political figures of the East and West with appropriate declarations denouncing the aggressive activity of American intelligence.

10. To prepare and publish in the bourgeois press, through available means, a number of articles on the activities of the CIA and its leaders on the following questions:

    a) about how A. DULLES used his position to promote his own enrichment. In particular, to demonstrate that DULLES gets big bribes from the "Lockheed" corporation for allocating contracts to produce reconnaissance planes. To indicate that the source of this information is the wife of a vice-president of "Lockheed" corporation and well-known American pilot Jacqueline COCHRAN, who allegedly leaked it in France on her way to the USSR in 1959;

    b) about the CIA's violation of traditional principles of non-partisanship on the part of the USA intelligence service. To demonstrate that in reality the CIA is the tool of reactionary circles in the Republican Party, that it ignores the Senate, the Congress and public opinion in the country;

    c) about the unjustifiably large expenditures of the CIA on its staff and its multitudinous agents and about the failure of its efforts to obtain information on the military-economic potential and scientific-technical achievements of the Soviet Union;

    d) about the unprecedented fact that the American embassy in Budapest is hosting Cardinal MINDSZENTY, furnishing evidence that the Americans are flouting the sovereign rights of the Hungarian People's Republic and demonstrating the sloppy work of American intelligence that damages American prestige in the eyes of world public opinion;

e) about the CIA's flawed methods of preparing spy cadres in the [training] schools at Fort Jersey (South Carolina) and in Monterey (California). To draw special attention to futility of efforts by the CIA and by DULLES personally to build a reliable intelligence [network] with emigrants from the USSR and the countries of people's democracies. To present a list of names of American intelligence officers and agents who have refused to work for DULLES on political, moral and other grounds;

f) about utilization by the CIA leadership of senior officials from the State Department, including ambassadors, for sub-versive and intelligence operations that cause great harm to USA prestige. In particular, to cite the example of DULLES' use of American ambassador [to South Korea Walter P.] MCCONAUGHY in subversive plans in Cambodia and then in South Korea;

g) about the activities of American intelligence in West Berlin in covering officers of West German intelligence services with documents of American citizens.

11. To approach the state security leadership in countries of people's democracy requesting that they use available means to discredit the CIA and to compromise A. DULLES.

Asking for your agreement to aforementioned measures, CHAIRMAN OF THE COMMITTEE

[signature] (A. Shelepin)

CHAPTER 5

FLASHPOINT BERLIN

Under the post-Second World War settlement, Berlin was divided into four zones of occupation, three for the Western Allies (Britain, France and the United States) and an eastern sector controlled by Soviet Union. The city became the front line of the Cold War, with hundreds of spies bidding to steal secrets, gain advance warning of military operations (a particular concern for the Western Allies who feared a Soviet attack on West Berlin) and generally to spread disinformation to discredit the other side.

This document by the Stasi (*Staatssicherheit*), the much-feared East German State Security Police, outlines their assessment of the Western intelligence operations in East Berlin in 1958. The Stasi was kept busy by the many categories of potential recruits, from alleged Fascist sympathizers, to sailors who docked in both eastern and western ports, scientists attending conferences and refugees, with the latter posing a particular threat while the border between East and West Germany remained open and porous until the building of the Berlin Wall in 1961. The Stasi also commented on the spy apparatus used by Western agents, in particular the MINOX, a miniature camera with a telephoto lens, equally useful for photographing documents or military installations.

The "heavy blows" dealt to the Americans in 1956 to which the Stasi assessment refers was the discovery of the Berlin Tunnel, a 300-metre long shaft dug in 1954–55 by an Anglo-American team across the east–west demarcation line. Laced with microphones and devices to tap East German telephone cables, within a year it had

yielded over 40,000 hours of telephone conversations, including detailed information on Soviet and East German military formations. On
22 April 1956, however, the tunnel was discovered by Soviet and East
German soldiers. Dramatically, the wiretaps and microphones continued to work until the very end, providing an agonizing final piece of
intelligence for the Western operators. Yet all was not as it seemed.
The existence of the tunnel and Operation Gold, the intelligence-
gathering operation it drove, had been betrayed from the very start
by the MI6 defector George Blake. The "discovery" of the tunnel
merely showed that the KGB and Stasi had tired of their double
game. The amount of disinformation, which was laced within the
stream of genuine (if low-level) intelligence they had permitted to be
revealed, may never be known.

Berlin never ceased to be a flashpoint right until the end of the
Cold War. In May 1981, KGB chief Yuri Andropov announced   a
massive programme of surveillance, code-named Operation Ryan (an
acronym for *Raketno-Yadernoye Napadenie* or "Nuclear Missile Attack") in which KGB Residencies throughout Western countries were
instructed to monitor for signs that might indicate a nuclear attack
was about to be launched. In November 1983 the KGB decided that
NATO was about to launch a first nuclear strike under cover of an
exercise named Able Archer. Its telegram to all residencies (including
Berlin) is typical of Operation Ryan preparation, advising agents to
keep watch for what it believed would be signs of a NATO attack,
including a rise in blood donations and lights being kept on late at
government ministries.

STASI ASSESSMENT OF WESTERN INTELLIGENCE OPERATIONS IN BERLIN

November, 1958

East German Ministry of State Security (Stasi), 'New Methods of Operation of Western Secret Services'

I. The following material is based on experience of investigative
work of the last few months as well as information obtained from
the exchange of information with other responsible departments.

<u>Applies to all secret services:</u> [they] react to the political situation in each case – party and government.

For example:
- chemistry conference
- proposals USSR and GDR for the resolution of the West Berlin question

<u>Characteristic:</u>

Immediate reaction on the part of all intelligence services to proposals – particularly Americans and Federal Intelligence Service – Officers worried, confused – however, unlike politicians of the Western Powers they assessed the situation relatively realistically; that is to say: comprehensive re-ordering of their work.

    (a) foreigners and officers of the Federal Intelligence Service go to West Germany
    (b) general conversion to radio and preparation for war <u>important:</u> not only specialist radio operators;
    (c) use of the most modern technology;
    (d) covert addresses [in] West Germany, dead drop boxes, and smuggling routes on the Western state border and the sectoral borders.

II. <u>American secret service:</u>

Yank dealt heavy blows in 1956, work completely re-ordered, agents switched off, German employees dismissed.
Lie detector – extensive questionnaires stating parents, siblings, home – [two words blacked out]
Recruitment on mass basis.
Work transferred from West Berlin to West Germany. Already various offices transferred to Frankfurt/Main and Kassel.
[handwritten note: illegible name] and others – Kassel office with telephone numbers from West Berlin
New methods in recruitment, cooperation, communication of intelligence –
Equipping for war
Sails under other flags. [handwritten note: Schütz [name]]

Recruitment methods:

Recruitment – refugee GDR-citizens; West German citizens, who come as asylum-seekers to the GDR; 5th Column;

Railway-workers, lorry drivers, and sailors on internal waterways, who are employed in interzonal travel;

Scientists and GDR citizens, who visit West Germany. Sailors who dock in West German ports;

Refugees ask acquaintances and relatives to visit them in West Berlin, there introduce them to secret service.

Poles and Czechs who are staying in West Germany are supplied with forged travel visas. [handwritten note: name blacked out – Visa. Border region – DLB store for documents and technical aids]

Cooperation:

Personal meetings are no longer carried out in bars, only in cars and safehouses which are mostly unknown to the agents.

Permanent change (*wechsel*) of safehouses – personal meetings are limited as much as possible – <u>for example:</u> Brehmer – one year

Meetings in West Berlin with "PM 12" or plane from West Berlin to West Germany

<u>Tasks:</u> transmitted by radio [handwritten note: no radio traffic [illegible word] Brehmer] For example: Brehmer

Courier connection via DLB.

Communication of intelligence:

West German covert addresses have been given out to almost all agents. Addresses do not exist, post office workers take them out, spy reports written with invisible ink (tablets – almost all tablets suited to making invisible ink) are also encoded. [handwritten note: and typewritten]

To a greater degree agents are equipped with radio sets – deadline 28 May 1959, replacement sets stored in DLBs.

With the radio sets – taperecorders, radio signals are transmitted on to these, tape plays at <u>ten times</u> <u>normal speed</u> over the transmitter – therefore hard to locate.

Along the sectoral borders and Western state border smuggling routes for people and DLBs

Resident agents are equipped with radio-telephones – for example: [name of agent blacked out] [handwritten note: Schneeberg [illegible word] Aue]

Regional radio headquarters: Frankfurt/Main, Fulda, Offenbach. [Handwritten note: radio with tape and pencil – then illegible]

<u>Technical aids:</u>

beyond those already stated:

(a) <u>Cameras:</u> built into glasses case, into wristwatch, cigarette lighter, and fountain pen. Chiefly the Minox is used – automatic camera with telephoto lens for railway junction – for example: [name of agent blacked out]

(b) <u>Bugging equipment</u> BASA/microphone – e.g. [name of agent blacked out] Tapping of telephone cables on roads and in telephone exchange, bugging devices are attached to tape recorders which run for 24 hours. Bugging devices which are equipped with a transmitter have been installed in chandeliers and pocket torches. For example: [name of spy blacked out].

(c) Devices which record radioactive emissions fixed to railway tracks so as to detect uranium transports – for example: [name of spy blacked out]

(d) Transport of technical devices, codes, and instructions takes places in packaging materials which are in common use in the GDR, e.g. cans of beef, tins of paint, bars of chocolate, accordions, vacuum cleaners.

<u>III. British secret service:</u>

is divided in West Berlin into:

12 Berlin Intelligence Staff (BIS) carries out only military espionage – mostly groups, partly using army officers without experience of secret service work as members and Secret Intelligence Service (SIS) – carries out:

(a) military espionage
(b) economic and political espionage Fundamentally rejects the creation of espionage groups.

Base of both departments of the British secret service on the premises of the Reich sports ground (Olympic Stadium Prohibited Zone). They are directly responsible to the Prime Minister.

Recruitment methods:

Utterly rejects mass recruitment, chiefly makes use of refugees who write to their circle of acquaintances and relatives. [handwritten note: compare with [name blacked out] – direct work on the person in the GDR – summoned by means of letters.

In making recruitments the officers speak openly of the British secret service and as evidence that cooperation will be secure state that no British agents have yet been sentenced on the territory of the GDR, otherwise there would have been articles in the democratic press.

[They] eagerly recruit GM [Geheime Mitarbeiter: secret co-workers], GI [Geheime Informatoren: secret informants] or contacts of the MfS, tell agents to join the SED. [handwritten note: strongly working for "P-sources"]

Maintaining the connection

The agents are mainly given telephone numbers 93 51 40 or 45. When calling these numbers from a public telephone in West Berlin the caller's money is returned after the conversation ends.
[handwritten note: respect when calling – call from [then illegible]]
When the exchange answers, the agent asks for an extension number given to him by the intelligence officer. However, these are agent numbers.

Meeting places: safehouses; cars; car-parks at night; [handwritten note: lorries – with perfectly installed meeting rooms – drive around Berlin – illegible word (cover)]; occasionally also in barracks and in the Olympic Stadium – meetings in bars are ruled out.

Furthermore, it is to be noted that the British secret service uses the wives of agents as couriers.

The conduct of espionage:

Infiltrates agents on long-term basis into state apparatus and party organizations and mass organizations; tells them to appear progressive, to join the SED.

Lets agents report orally using microphones,

Information written on Japanese tissue paper, original documents in briefcases with secret compartments.

Gives agents radio sets, however they are not yet in operation, only in case of war, DLBs also only for case of war.

Cover addresses have not yet appeared. [handwritten note: West Germany]

Camera built into petrol cans and briefcases.

IV. French secret service:

Sûreté National – organizes counter-espionage – above all [against the] MfS – [Unger [name]] West Berlin, Müllerstraße, uses violence in interrogations.

DR/Marine – works on Baltic coast – chiefly via Hamburg.

DR/SR: (a) army (b) air force (c) political and economic espionage

Strict separation of responsibility.

Main base in Germany: Baden-Baden.

West Berlin Quartier Napoleon – Reinickendorf, Kurt-Schumacher-Damm – Use German employees for recruitment and introduction

Cooperation chiefly with French officers.

Since [Soviet] Note on Berlin use of German employees on a greater scale.

French are making preparations for withdrawal. Equipping agents with radio sets.

Recruitment methods:

Zoo Station – black market dealer in optical goods – [handwritten note: House of the East German Homeland] – refugee camps about refugees (*Fluchtlingslager uber Republikfluchtige*) – [two words blacked out] – [handwritten note: exploitation of "Heimatverbände" – revanche].

Aids:

Japanese tissue paper (*Seidenpapier*)– shoes with hollow sole –
radio sets – winder and board which opens out as well as Morse
key. [handwritten note: [agent] does not need to be a radio operator]
Radio sets with tape just like the Americans.

Communication of intelligence:

DLBs, covert addresses in West Germany, couriers – personal meetings in safehouses and bars – radio connections.

Characteristic features

French secret service is currently generous with financial resources –
pays in advance monthly salary for one year, makes agents buy motor-
bikes and radio sets.

V. Federal Intelligence Service (BND):

1. Structure:

Change in the structure (1. Intelligence collection, 2. Sabotage –
Subversion and 3. Counter-espionage)
Now: 1. Spying [handwritten note: Near intelligence collection:
GDR; Deep intelligence collection: People's Democracies; Far intelligence collection: [USSR]; 2. War; 3. Intelligence collection and
work on hostile intelligence services.
[handwritten note: that is a more prominent feature of the BND's
character] That is to say: concentration now on war and hostile intelligence services.
Structure of offices (organization) remained as known up to now
Headquarters (GD – *Geheimdienst*), general agencies (GV – *General-
vertretungen*), district agencies (BV – *Bezirksvertretungen*), sub-agencies
(UV – *Untervertretungen*), local branches (FL – *Filialen*), and agent
controllers (VMF - *Vertrauensmannführer*).
Cover: as up to now (firms, trade representatives, and suchlike.)
[handwritten note: without (official) guard – only porters]

The BND's methods of activity:

(a) research and recruitment: main territory of research: West Germany, returnees, visitors to West Germany
Post and foreign offices – surveillance – collecting addresses
partly West Berlin – exploitation of offices which GDR citizens call at, e.g. Federal Support Offices (131-type pensions) etc.

Selection of recruitment candidates:

Up to now – chiefly Fascists, Wehrmacht and police officers Today – still the case – but Federal Intelligence Service seeks so-called "party faithful" – people who outwardly support the policy of the Party and state. [handwritten note: compare [name blacked out] – exploitation of grievance and compromising material]

Recruitment:

Known up to now – German theme – reunification of Germany among other phrases – activity in Nazi Germany revealed
New line: activity in Nazi Germany not revealed – if it is, then flag not revealed.
[handwritten note: general testing by means of 08 tasks, then P-sources (Weinderlich [name])]

(b) Working methods with agent networks:

1953-1956 offices (Fl) in West Berlin – severe blows by MfS
Transfer of all official offices to West Germany "to the secure hinterland."
Officers of the Federal Intelligence Service only now come to West Berlin for meetings. Constant changing of meeting places (hotels), e.g. [name blacked out]
Transfer to city districts located far from one another, only now partly in bars. [handwritten note: drives in taxis of more [illegible word]]
Instruction:
meetings also in West Germany
reduce number of meetings.

That is to say: the work from West Germany of the Federal Intelligence Service will increase in future.

(c) Methods of communicating intelligence:

Secret text [(ST)] process – covert addresses – [handwritten note: ST – Blue] particularly covert addresses in West Germany/water pressure process, drying process with prepared paper.

The peculiarities of covert addresses in West Germany: addresses of people who do not exist or second address (forwarding job) covert address passes on all messages to a second address – post office boxes and storage card – likewise second address.

- giving of instructions by means of films

13 points – economic spy.

15 points – political spy.

19 points – military spy.

21 points – military/economic spy.

- warning calendar (*Warnkalender*) handed over on films.
- increased laying of DLBs round Berlin and above all towards West Germany (motorway, railway lines)

[handwritten note: compare [deleted] telephone smuggling, secret service smuggling (channels and [illegible word])

- dispatch of parcels (parcel of biscuits) with money and intelligence on type-through paper (ST process) to second person.

Particular novelty – supplying all agents with radio sets – that is to say: transmitter–extremely small – with a winder/figures–duration of a normal transmission 20–30 seconds – "radio operator" does not need to be a radio expert.

reception devices: (shortwave converter) – attachment to radio with headphones – to receive instructions, whereby each operator receives: key, date, time of day, and time when headquarters will repeat [message].

(speech traffic – not machine)

Types of radio sets: "Eisenach," "Rema/800," "Dominante," "Stradivari/E9" and all sets with 2 loudspeakers.

Transports and hiding places:

Transport concealed in tins of preserved food from HO [*Handelsorganisation*: a state-owned network of shops and hotels], even unopened, has been maintained up to recent instructions. Children's toy – like cars and toy railway sets etc.

Utensils (pocket mirror) and cigarettes etc.

[Handwritten note: petrol cans – paint tins and some use with set parcel with pieces of clothing pieces of clothing in general]

Couriers:

There are specific instructions for selection and collaboration

For example: people who travel a lot (professionally), long-distance drivers, sailors, and suchlike, sales representatives, courier material not to be concealed on body, concealment during transport must offer the chance of abandoning the material easily.

(e) Other technical aids:

MINOX cameras

– Robot Star and Robot Junior with cable release and powerful tele-photo lens. Particularly during observation of MfS offices and officers.

3. Particular installations under attack:

Economic espionage against key parts of the people's economy (for example: chemistry, coal, energy, or big construction sites – Rostock harbour)

[handwritten note: see in connection with returnees]

Military espionage – all installations of the Soviet army and NVA [*Nationale Volksarmee:* the East German army.]

Stepped-up activity against the MfS and the organs subordinate to it. Aim: to penetrate, study, spy, "play games," smash existing IM [*Inoffizielle Mitarbeiter:* informants] groups.

Also spying on officers of MfS by means of observations, investigations, conversations, bar visits, drinking bouts, and suchlike.

Introduction of compromised MfS employees to secret service.

Conclusions:

1.   consistent political instruction of officers; each officer – each department must [form] from this corresponding conclusions for investigative work.

2. increases sharing of experience – give more attention to operational evaluation.
3. evaluation of investigation cases – more attention to presentation of evidence. Counter-espionage uses too little operational technology to obtain official evidence.

    for example: photographing meetings by means of an observer. Case [name blacked out] – operational combination tank Case [name blacked out] – [handwritten: (photographed handing over spying equipment)] therefore important: as the intelligence service now instructs its agents in interrogations to require evidence to be presented [handwritten: e.g. arrest order e.g. [name blacked out]] – no basis for arrest without confession.

    [handwritten: informants' information: show evidence – otherwise no confession]

    previously: MfS would make use of beatings and other physical means – agents thereby intimidated – the interrogator impressed by correct behaviour – confession.
4. All members of Departments IX, VII, M, XIV to be instructed about opportunities for concealment – most meticulous inspection of all objects found on spies – more use to be made of Department K – [handwritten note: quartz lamp, magnets, X-rays]

    personal participation of interrogators in house searches.
5. In the future more agent radio operators (every spy can possess a radio set) – question every agent about knowledge of radio – conversations about this with controllers, training and technical devices received – if it is suspected that the agents possess a radio, search with a detection device.
6. Question migrants from West Germany whether they have been recruited.

THE EAST GERMANS/RUSSIANS DISCOVER A
WESTERN WIRE-TAP TUNNEL EXTENDING INTO
EAST BERLIN

15 August 1956

DISCOVERY BY THE SOVIETS OF THE TUNNEL

Analysis of all available evidence – traffic passing on the target cables, conversations recorded from a microphone installed in the tap chamber, and vital observations from the site – indicates that the Soviet discovery of •••••••• [the tunnel] was purely fortuitous and was not the result of a penetration of the •••••••• agencies concerned, a security violation, or testing of the lines by the Soviets or East Germans. A description of the events leading to these conclusions is contained in this paper.

Following heavy rains in the Berlin area a number of telephone and telegraph cables were flooded and began to fault between Karlshorst and Mahlow on the night of 16 April 1956. The first major fault was discovered on cable FK 151 at Wassmannsdorf on 17 April. The fault was repaired by cutting the defective stretch of cable and replacing a 3000 meter length with a temporary replacement cable. Between 17 and 22

(Page 2 missing from the original document)

continued This general situation was noted by personnel at the site who checked the tap on the morning of 19 April and found it to be in good condition with no faults present. Berlin notified Headquarters of this fact on the evening of 20 April, noting, "available precautions taken including primary one of crossing fingers."

Throughout 20 April Soviet operators at Karlshorst, the Mahlow cable chamber, and Zossen/Wuensdorf checked FK 150 pairs carrying circuits serving high ranking officials and made switches where necessary or possible. Nothing was said concerning the testing being conducted to discover the faults or work being done by a Soviet labor force lent to the Germans to assist in digging up bad stretches of cable. On 21 April a Karlshorst technician told a colleague in Zossen/Wuensdorf the FK 150 had not yet been repaired and that another two days' work would probably be necessary to clear up the trouble. Testing and rerouting of circuits were stepped up during the evening of 21 April, and the Soviets showed considerable concern over the failure of the Moscow–GSFG Air Warning telegraph channel which had been transferred to FK 150 on 17 April. Lt. Colonel Vyunik, Chief of the GSFG Signal Center at Wuensdorf, telephoned Major Alpatov, Chief of the Karlshorst Signal Center, at his apartment to inform him of the failure of the Air Warning circuit. They agreed that communications had to be established before morning and Alpatov left for his duty station.

There is no significant information available on the actual progress of the testing and repair program proper from 0300 hours on 20 April to 0050 hours on 22 April. On the basis of available information, however, it seems probable that (a) the testing program continued north until a fault was located near the site and a decision was made to replace an entire section of cable which embraced the tap site; or (b) the repeated faulting coupled with the age and physical condition of FK 150 led the opposition to the conclusion that the only effective remedy was to replace the cable, section by section, and that this program was inaugurated somewhere south of our site and continued northward until the tap was discovered.

At approximately 0050 hours on 22 April, 40 or 50 men were seen on the east side of Schoenefelder Allee, deployed along the entire area observable from our installation, digging at three to five foot intervals over the location of the cable and, incidentally, the tap chamber. At approximately 0200 hours the top of the tap chamber was discovered, and at 0210 Russian speech was heard from the microphone in the tap chamber. The first fragments of speech indicated that the discovery of the tap chamber aroused no suspicion among those present. A small hole was broken in the tap chamber roof permitting limited visual observation of the chamber, and a Soviet captain was brought to the spot. After some discussion all agreed that the discovery was a manhole covering a repeater point, and the working crew began enlarging the hole to gain access to the "repeater point."

While the working party was uncovering the tap chamber, Major Alpatov and Lt. Colonel Vyunik discussed the communications situation in a rambling telephone conversation at approximately 0230 hours. They indicated relief at the restoration of Air Warning Communications with Moscow, and Vyunik went on to express suspicion about the continued trouble on FK 150. In context it appears that this suspicion was directed at the failure of the Germans to clear up the difficulties on FK 150 once and for all. In any event, Alpatov clearly did not share his colleague's doubts. The general tone of this conversation was relaxed and casual, completely in keeping with the character of the two men, both of whom we know well. The conversation appears to be a clear indication that, as of 0230 hours on 22 April, neither of these responsible officers was aware of the existence of the tap.

Meanwhile back at the site the work of enlarging a hole to give full access to the tap chamber continued. At approximately 0250 hours an unidentified Soviet Colonel arrived on the scene, presumably in response to a request for guidance by the working party. The Colonel did not appear to be a signal officer since he took no active part in the investigation and remained on the scene only for a short time. Having enlarged the hole in the tap chamber roof, the workers saw for the first time the cables and the trap door on the floor of the chamber. They assumed the trap door to be "some sort of box" and had no suspicion of the true nature of the installation. At approximately 0300 hours barriers were erected to keep inquisitive onlookers away from the excavation and it was suggested that someone be sent to the Signal Directorate, presumably to obtain relevant cable data. At the same time the first German voice was heard, in conversation with a German-speaking Russian. The German stated that two trucks must have passed the spot without locating it. The Russian answered that "Soviet troops are coming as well," and added that they must wait "until morning" for the decision as to what further work would be undertaken.

While these developments were taking place, Vyunik held a telecon with the Air Warning Center in Moscow in which he referred to the move of the GSFG Air Warning Center and discussed, in detail, communication arrangements necessitated by this move. This revealing teleconference tends to support other evidence indicating that as of 0300 hours the true nature of the installation had still not been established.

The work of excavation continued, and fragments of conversation connected with it were picked up by the tap chamber microphone. A German-speaking Russian commented that "somebody has come from there and there are fewer workers there," suggesting that similar work was in progress at another point. The Russian gave instructions that nothing in the installation was to be touched. A German remarked that the chamber might be connected with sewage work and proposed that plans of the sewage system be obtained from the responsible authorities. The Russian answered that they already had this information and that the plans showed "that chamber" to be 120 meters away from this point. At about 0320 hours, when still more of the tap chamber was revealed and a better view of the interior obtained, those present began to speculate vaguely about its exact nature and the time of its construction. One of the Soviets, probably an officer, suggested that it might have been built during the war, possibly for "Vhe Che" (Russian abbreviation for "high frequency transmission," but used loosely to denote anything connected with secure communications.) Shortly after 0330 hours, the Soviets left the site by motor vehicle, presumably to report their findings. For approximately one and one-half hours – from 0330 to 0500 – no sounds or voices were recorded.

At approximately 0415 hours Vyunik telephoned Alpatov's apartment in Karlshorst and asked Alpatov if he had spoken with General Dudakov, Chief Signal Officer, GSFG. Alpatov said that he had, that he was getting dressed, and that he would go to his signal center as soon as possible. Vyunik told Alpatov to telephone him at the GSFG frame room at Zossen/Wuensdorf, adding, "When we speak we must do so carefully. We know what the matter is, so we will speak carefully." This indicated clearly that by 0415 hours the GSFG Signal Directorate and General Dudakov, the Chief Signal Officer, had been informed of the discovery of the •••••••• [tunnel tap] chamber, viewed it with extreme suspicion, and planned to reroute circuits passing over the target cables. This coincides neatly with the departure from the tap site of the Soviets at 0330. At 0630 Vyunik telephoned Alpatov at the Karlshorst Signal Center and informed him that Lt. Colonel Zolochko, Deputy Chief of the Lines Department, GSFG, had left Wuensdorf at 0625 to go "there." Vyunik, in a resigned tone, then added that all that remained for him and Alpatov to do was to sit and wait.

In due course Lt. Colonel Zolochko arrived at the site, accompanied by an unnamed Colonel and Captain Bartash, the Commander of the working party. By this time the Soviets apparently had brought circuit diagrams to the site and were aware of the pair allocations on the affected cables. There was considerable discussion of the discovery, and one of the crew actually entered the chamber and made a superficial and inconclusive examination. Shortly afterwards the statement, "the cable is tapped," was made for the first time on the scene.

At about this time (0635 hours) Lt. Vyunik telephoned Major Alpatov and asked whether he had received the "task" and whether its meaning was clear. Alpatov replied that he had received and understood the assignment. Speaking in unusually vague terms, Vyunik instructed Alpatov to take over two low-frequency channels, presumably provided by the KGB signals organization. (These channels would provide telephone communications between Berlin and Wuensdorf via overhead line and would by-pass the tapped cables.) Vyunik added that they could continue necessary technical discussions on the new facilities.

Although teletype traffic continued until the tap wires were cut – at 1535 hours on Sunday afternoon – the last telephone call of any interest was placed sometime between 0800 and 0900 hours on 22 April, when an agitated General speaking from Marshal Grechko's apartment attempted to contact Colonel Kotsyuba, who was then acting for General Dibrova, Berlin Commandant. Unable to locate Kotsyuba, the General talked to Colonel Pomozanovskii, Chief of Staff of the Berlin Garrison, stressing the urgency of his call. Pomozanovskii promised to find Kotsyuba at once and get him to return the call. The return call was not intercepted, but there appears to be no doubt that Marshal Grechko had by this time been informed of the discovery and wished to discuss it with Colonel Kotsyuba. A few telephone calls were attempted after this, but the operators refused to place the calls, and in one case a Karlshorst operator said, "I won't put you through to anyone. Don't ring, that's all. I won't answer you any more. It's in the order."

Between 0700 and 0800 hours a number of additional Soviet officers arrived at the excavation, including Colonel Gusev of the KGB Signals Regiment. A Russian-speaking German was heard to remark that a "commission" was expected, and a Soviet officer said that they would await the arrival of this commission before making a decision as to what the next step would be. In answer to a question as to whether anything should be disconnected, the same officer stated that nothing should be done beyond making motion pictures of the chamber. He added, however, that the hole providing access to the chamber should be enlarged and a detailed inspection should be carried out. The general discussion continued, and the possibility of some form of explosive booby trap in the chamber was discussed at some length. There was widespread belief that the trap door, which in fact provided access to the tunnel proper, was a "box" or "battery box" possibly involving a booby trap. One of the Soviet officers, probably Zolochko, suggested that, after everything had been carefully noted and recorded, a grappling iron could be attached to the "box" in order to tear it away. "If there is no explosion," he said, "then we can calmly go ahead and deal with it."

Several individuals, presumably German cable splicers, agreed that the cables were fully tapped and discussed the method employed. They agreed that it must have been done in such a way as to render the tap undetectable by measurements, although one of them failed to understand why the actual cutting of the cables was not detected. He added that at that time "everyone must have been quite drunk." The Germans continued to speculate on the nature of the "box" and about the means of access to the tap chamber. One of them said, "They themselves must have some means of entering this place, but naturally it's highly improbable that they have constructed a passage for getting from here to there!"

Some of those present apparently believed that the tap was an old one and had been abandoned due to recent faults on the cable. During this discussion the microphone was twice noted, but was not recognized for what it was. In the first instance the speaker said, "That is not a microphone," and in the second it was described as "a black ball."

The general discussion continued, with speculation as to the nature of the "battery box" and with several comments that it should be possible to identify the tappers "from the make of the materials" and the techniques employed. While the Germans began work enlarging the hole around the tap chamber, the Soviets discussed in some detail the order in which technical experts and administrative representatives would carry out their inspection. The Soviets identified the lead-off cable as "not ours," indicating that after the inspection they planned to disconnect the lead-off cable and to "check how far it goes from here" – probably by means of electrical measurements. It is evident that at this time (approximately 1130 hours) the Soviets and Germans were still unaware of the existence of the tunnel, the means of access to the tap chamber, or those responsible for the tap.

At approximately 1145 hours one of the German crew was heard to exclaim, "The box is an entry to a shaft!"

From the tenor of the ensuing conversation it would seem that a small hole had been made near the still-intact trap door. The Germans debated the removal of the trap door, but continued to work at and around it despite the alternate suggestion that "we should open up the road opposite until we reach the cable or the shaft." By approximately 1230 they had removed the hinges and entered the lower part of the tap chamber. The padlock which secured the trap door from below was examined and was identified as "of English origin." Failing to open the door separating the tap chamber from the equipment chamber, the Germans, after approximately twenty minutes, broke a hole through the wall and gained visual access to the equipment chamber, which they described as "a long passage." By 1300 they evidently had enlarged the access hole and described "a completed installation – a telephone exchange.......An installation for listening in [Abhoeranlage]."

Additional motion pictures were made and frequent exclamations of wonder and admiration were heard. At 1420 a Soviet Colonel, probably Zolochko; a person addressed as Nikolai Ivanovich, probably Major Alpatov; and a Gaptain, presumably Bartash, entered the chamber and discussed the method used by the tappers in gaining access to the cables. Zolochko evidently still believed that this was done "from above." Conversations indicated that the joint Soviet-German commission, mentioned earlier, had already visited the site and established the nature of the installation without going into technical details.

Measurements of parts of the interior were then taken, discussion of the installation became general, and the participants clearly indicated that the means of access and full implications of the operation were finally appreciated. Conversations reflected that all present realized that the planning of the tunnel approach to the cables must have necessitated a very detailed study of relevant maps and plans. The stress to which the roof of the chambers would be subjected and the necessity of preparing the lead-off cables beforehand were mentioned, and a German was heard to exclaim, "It must have cost a pretty penny." A Russian-speaking German added, admiringly, "How neatly and tidily they have done it." It was decided that work on the tunnel must have been carried out during the day when the sound of the street traffic would drown any noise, whereas the actual tapping was done "during the night, between one and two o'clock, when the traffic on the cables is slight."

One of the Germans rather indignantly exclaimed, "What a filthy trick. And where you would least expect it." — to which another replied, "Unless one had seen it for oneself, nobody would believe it."

Between 1515 and 1530 hours the tap wires were cut, and at about 1545 the attention of the Germans began to concentrate on the microphone itself. One of them assumed it to be an "alarm device – probably a microphone," to give warning of approaching motor traffic, and added that it ought to be photographed. At 1550 hours work began on dismantling the microphone. Shortly afterward the microphone went dead and, after 11 months and 11 days, the operational phase of •••••••• [THE TUNNEL] was completed.

KGB ASSESSMENT OF NATO
NUCLEAR WAR PREPARATIONS

Reference No 373/PR/52

Top Secret
Copy No. 1
Attachment 1

Permanent Operational Assignment
to discover NATO Preparations for
a Nuclear Attack on the USSR

Section 1 – Immediate tasks of Residencies for Collecting Information and Organising their Work

1.   Collect data about places where Government officials and members of their families are evacuated. Identify possible routes and methods of evacuation. Make suggestions about ways of organising a watch to be kept on preparation and actual evacuation.

Time limit: 3rd quarter [by 30 September 1983]

2.   Identify the location of specially equipped Civil Defence shelters or premises which could if necessary be used as shelters (underground garages and depots, basements, tunnels) and arrange for a periodical check on their state of preparedness to accommodate the population at a particular time.

Time limit: 3rd quarter [by 30 September 1983]

      Report to Centre immediately if shelters are being taken out of storage or a start is being made on preparing certain premises for accommodation of the population.

3.   One important sign that preparations are beginning for RYAN could be increased purchases of blood from donors and the prices paid for it and extension of the network of reception centres, since the treatment of burns (the most widespread injury in a nuclear explosion) requires blood transfusions in very considerable quantity. In this context, discover the location of several blood-donor reception centres, and find out how they operate and the price of the blood donated, and record any changes.

Time limit: 2nd quarter [by 30 June 1983]

If there is an unexpectedly sharp increase in the number of stationary and mobile blood donor centres and in the prices paid, report at once to the Centre.

4.   Put forward proposals for organising a watch on individual civil defence installations. Time limit: 2nd quarter [by 30 June 1983]

5.   Identify several places which are most frequently visited outside working hours by employees of institutions and installations connected with taking and implementing decisions regarding RYAN, including military personnel. Put forward your views about the possibility of regular observation of the places selected.
Time limit: 2nd quarter [by 30 June 1983]

6.   Keep under regular observation the most important government institutions, headquarters and other installations involved in preparation for RYAN. Send a list of immediate targets of observation to the Centre. Ascertain the 'normal level of activity' of these targets in and out of working hours, i.e. the outward signs of their daily activity in a normal situation (differences in the number of cars collected there in the daytime and the evening, and in the number of lighted windows in and out of working hours, and activity round these targets on non-working days). Find out, on the basis of the 'normal level' ascertained, any changes in the indicators during special conferences, when there is a crisis situation (cars collected there out of hours, an increase in the number of lighted windows at night in comparison with the 'normal level', or increased activity on non-working days).

7.   Set a regular watch for any significant changes in the police administration system and the activity of the special [i.e. security and intelligence] services in regard to Soviet citizens and institutions, which may be associated with preparation for RYAN.

On points 6 and 7 inform Centre of the existence or absence of any changes of this kind regularly – once every two weeks.

Section II – Principal Prospective Directions for the Residency to Pursue its Work of Collecting the Information Needed to Discover the Adversary's Preparations for RYAN

1.   Detailed description of the nature of measures being carried out in your country of residence by NATO headquarters and

agencies, American representations and military installations located there at a time of immediate preparation by the USA and NATO for RYAN.

2. Analysis of the possibility of co-opting existing agents to work on uncovering preparation for RYAN and of using all available resources for this purpose.

3. Identifying and studying with a view to subsequent cooption for collaboration, a cadre of people associated with preparing and implementing the decision about RYAN, and also a group of people, including service and technical personnel, who might be informed of the fact that this or that measure is being taken in preparation for RYAN, even if they do not know its objective or purport (the official chauffeurs of individuals involved in the decision about RYAN, those working in the operating services of installations connected with processing and implementing the decision about RYAN, and communications staff involved in the operation and interaction of these installations).

4. Studying the possibilities of organising systematic observation of persons associated with taking the decision about RYAN and those who might be informed of the preparation of such a decision.

5. Uncovering the lines of communication used for preparing for RYAN, their terminal points, switchboards and system of operating in normal conditions and in an emergency situation, technical characteristics and the possibility of interception.

6. Assessment of opportunities for keeping watch for changes in the pattern of operation of government institutions which are involved in taking political decisions regarding RYAN, and are responsible for the country's military preparedness and for contacts with NATO allies.

7. Collecting data about plans for preparing the special [intelligence and security] services for a particular time and for possible action at that time. Studying facilities for organising a systematic watch to be kept for changes in the operating routine of the central establishments of the special services.

8. Identifying the places where the country's leading military and political figures, and state institutions, including personnel from the central apparatus of the special services, are to be evacuated.

9. Identifying possible routes and methods of evacuating military and political leaders and state institutions. Studying the possibilities of discovering promptly when evacuation is in progress.
10. Gathering data about the location of control centres and headquarters of civil defence forces, shelters, depots and training posts of the civil defence system. Assessment of the possibilities of discovering immediate preparation of the civil defence system for war.
11. Defining the possibility of finding out with present resources what measures are being taken to bring military installations, which are accessible to our observation into a state of heightened operational preparedness. Collecting information about the main residential and recreational centres of the services, hospitals and other installations closely connected with military bases and headquarters.
12. Assessing the degree of likelihood that the heads of national churches and of international church organisations, and the leadership and institutions of the Vatican abroad would be aware of preparation for a nuclear attack and clarifying possibilities of obtaining information about RYAN from these circles.
13. Bearing in mind the very considerable knowledge possessed by the heads of international and the larger national banks, examine the possibility of obtaining information about RYAN from such circles.

The Residency must organise its work in a planned manner on the questions which have been enumerated. Please keep the Centre regularly informed as information is obtained.

No. 374/PR/52

CHAPTER 6

SUSPECT AGENTS AND DEFECTORS

Instructions for Checking a Suspect Agent

Defectors are the nightmare of any intelligence organization. Those who remain in their position, as "defectors in place" provide a stream of information to a hostile power often from the very heart of the intelligence establishment. The "Cambridge Spy Ring" of Guy Burgess, Kim Philby and Donald Maclean operated for decades in senior positions in MI6 and the Foreign Office, including – in Philby's case – as MI6 liaison officer to the CIA and FBI in Washington. Unmasking them was made more difficult by the ability of each to warn the others of potential evidence against them. The KGB also suffered its share of damaging defectors, beginning in 1945 with Igor Gouzenko, a cypher clerk in the Soviet Embassy in Ottawa, whose information led to the arrest of Alan Nunn May and other spies working on the American atomic bomb project. The defection in 1961 of Anatoli Golitsyn, a KGB officer posted to Helsinki revealed the identities of dozens of Soviet agents, and led to the final unmasking of Kim Philby and the exposure of John Vassal, who had leaked intelligence to the Soviets from the British Admiralty.

It is no wonder then that the KGB (and other intelligence agencies) developed elaborate protocols to detect potential traitors and then to discover the extent of any network of defectors. When Oleg Penkovsky was identified as a defector after being spotted by the KGB exchanging documents with an MI6 contact, he was permitted to remain free, but under observation, for several months, allowing

Soviet intelligence to arrest his courier, the British businessman
Greville Wynne, in November 1962.

The KGB handbook advises careful scrutiny of the suspected
defector, arranging for the provision of "test containers" containing
sensitive documents which were to be passed on to another contact
unopened or of sealed letters which, again, the agent was supposed
to hand on unread. When these were recovered by the KGB, any
evidence of tampering or, indeed, any sign that the intelligence (presumably faked) was being acted upon by a foreign intelligence agency,
would be proof of the defection. More generally, close attention was
to be paid to any new and suspicious contacts made by the agent,
or changes in his family circumstance that might render him open to
blackmail by a foreign power. Routine bugging of the agent's apartment was also recommended to root out traitors. The fate of a captured defector was severe. Although the United States only executed
two spies (Julius and Ethel Rosenberg who had betrayed America's
atom secrets), Soviet defectors, when caught, were invariably shot.

KGB BASIC INSTRUCTIONS FOR CHECKING
AGENTS AND DEEP STUDY TARGETS AMONG
FOREIGNERS ABROAD

gzh–1   Top Secret
No 6631/X   Copy No 1
24 May 1978

COPENHAGEN
To: Comrade KORIN [LYUBIMOV]

We are forwarding herewith a report entitled 'Basic methods for
conducting checks on agents, and deep study targets among foreigners abroad', which has been prepared by the appropriate sub-section
of our service for possible use when planning checking measures on
the existing agent network, future targets of deep study and operational contacts.

Attachment on 16 pages, Secret No 151/2–6650 DM.
[Ms note]

Please inform all members of the operational staff. This material must be used when drafting the relevant proposals.

KORIN [LYUBIMOV]

6.6.78

SECRET

Copy No 1

Attachment to No 6631/X

Basic Methods for Checking Agents and Deep Study Targets Among Foreigners Abroad

The following are the basic and essential requirements by which Residencies must be guided in their daily operational practice in order guarantee security in their work with foreign agents:

1. The checking of an agent apparatus must be a continuous process, irrespective of the basis on which the agent was recruited, the degree of confidence we have in him or the length of time he has been collaborating with us;

2. Well thought-out agent checks must be carried out *not more than once a year* and, should any doubts regarding reliability crop up a complex of special checks using operational-technical methods must be implemented;

3. The above-mentioned checks must pursue strictly defined aims, conform to the specific circumstances and realistic possibilities, as well as being based on the results of an analysis of all available material and an assessment of previous work with the agent.

The basic aim of these checks must be the acquisition of reliable data enabling conclusions to be drawn concerning the following problems:

– whether the person being checked has links with hostile special services and is acting on their behalf (check for plants);

– whether the person being checked is a deep study target for hostile Special Services (check for loss of cover);

– whether he is sincerely co-operating with us and making active use of his intelligence potential (check on sincerity);

In practical operational work the methods listed below for studying and carrying out checks on agents may be used.

I. Methods of conducting checks without the use of agents

1. *The studying and checking of an agent in the course of personal contact between him and a case officer.*

- By accumulating biographical and character data on the agent and by rechecking this periodically;
- By regularly highlighting any changes in the agent's political or ideological views as well as changes in his work – or social circumstances; a realistic appraisal of the reasons for his collaborating with us and his intelligence potential;
- By determining his reactions to tasks of an operational and test nature, to discussions on his personal life, his sources of information etc;
- By collecting data on the agent's close contacts and the subsequent checking of these through existing means;
- Any change in the agent's family circumstances, inter-relationships within the family; his lifestyle;
- By his observance of security measures in performing intelligence tasks, the clandestinity of his behaviour;
- By periodical checks as to how the agent is observing the conditions for contacting and cover-stories concerning his intelligence activity.

2. *The checking of an agent through official means*

Various kinds of official sources of information comprising institutional and biographical information on governmental, political and commercial personalities may be used:

- telephone directories;
- parliamentary, party and company directories;
- newspapers and journals;
- official archives and libraries;
- Police Department bulletins;

– the facilities offered by Chambers of Commerce, banks, companies and brokers;
– electoral registers;
– population census material;
– professional directories.

3. *Checking a target of study through his connections and contacts*

– The case officer or illegal makes unconscious use of his neutral cover connections and contacts to collect information and crosscheck individual facts or biographical data about the target of study;
– the carrying out of analogous work using agents and co-opted collaborators of Soviet nationality, and also in isolated cases case officers' wives. The specific task and methods of carrying it out must have been carefully planned beforehand for these people.

In all cases where connections and contacts are used for checking it is essential to be extremely careful and to have a well thought-out cover story for the conversations in order to conceal the real reasons for our interest in the target of study.

4. *Checks in which only Residency officials or illegals take part*

– By instigating checks at places of work and residencies of the object of study by means of personal visits or with the aid of the telephone;
– Arranging for surveillance to be placed on the object of study to check his pattern of work; to identify the places he visits, discover his contacts etc. The implementation of such measures in relation to agents must inevitably be combined with tasks which have been specially worked out for them and which will permit the monitoring of their actions;
– The mounting of counter-surveillance on the object of study on previously stipulated routes or routes we know he uses, with the object of discovering any signs that he is under surveillance by hostile special services;
– The use of various operational-technical aids to check agents (will be treated below)

5. *Checks through an analysis of the intelligence received*

The following considerations must be taken into account when arranging and implementing such checks:

– It is essential to analyse not only the contents of the material but also the nature of the documents – whether originals or copies. First and foremost, measures must be taken to amplify and cross-check data about the sources, the times and circumstances of the acquisition of the intelligence; also a comparison of the material may be made alongside past and other original documents from the corresponding institution, checking typewriter prints etc;
– Side by side with a regular evaluation of the importance and authenticity of individual items of intelligence it is essential to assess the subject's intelligence work as a whole over a specific period of time (a quarter, half-year, full year etc), as this will enable a survey to be made of the overall value of the information and its trends, and will also establish more accurately which of the material from the source is not corroborated by the further course of events.

6. *Checking an agent by the imposition of special tasks*

The following variants may be considered as examples of the diversity of checks which are possible under this heading:

– Setting the agent the task of collecting basic information and character data on a number of people about whom we already have sufficiently full and reliable knowledge;
– The checking or collection of information on events, facts and personalities, partly or completely fictitious (if there is no suspicion of possible links between the agent and hostile special services);
– The obtaining of information (documentary or de visu), already well known to the Centre from other sources;
– Preparing for the agent a task which it is outside his competence to fulfil without recourse to specialists or to counter-intelligence (if he is in contact with it). For example:

a) To visit restricted areas and collect data on such targets as can only be correctly described by someone having specialist knowledge and practical skills;

b) To send him to a country which has difficult operating condi-
    tions to meet a 'valuable agent' within a tight time limit, provided
    that local conditions make this practically impossible to accom-
    plish without the help of special organs;

– The imposition of a test assignment which forces the adversary to
  perform specific actions thereby exposing himself to monitoring
  from our side, for example:

a) To carry out a check on a specific person in order to collect infor-
    mation about him (places of work and residence, hours of work,
    the routes he follows, places he frequents etc), an analysis of which
    must lead the adversary to suspect that we intend to re-establish
    a lost contact with him and subsequently to organize surveillance
    in case of a possible change in the status of this person;

b) To ensure the departure by air of an undercover agent from the
    country in possession of valuable material (possibility of supple-
    mentary checks on the aircraft flight in question or delaying the
    aircraft);

– the imposition of tasks whose fulfilment would involve matters of
  principle which the agent would not be able to decide by himself
  without consultations with hostile special services (assuming he is
  in contact with them) and this would show itself in his conduct
  and reaction to such assignments.

   An indispensable condition for the successful use of this method of checking is that the tasks should appear natural, realistic, well
thought-out, and should flow from the whole course of previous
work with agent.

II. Checking with the help of agents

When using agents for preparing and carring out checks on targets of study, the following basic requirements must be rigorously
observed:

1. Do not allow one agent to be aware of others;
2. The target under scrutiny must not discover the measures being
    taken by the Residency for checking him;
3. The agent to whom the checking is entrusted must be reliable.

   The following are possible options in the use of agents for checking purposes:

- Collecting information about the target of study about his life,
  business and social activity, contacts, political views, personal and
  business qualities, intelligence potential etc and also for cross-
  checking individual facts or events from his life and activities;
- Acquiring specific information from parallel agents enabling material obtained from the person under study to be cross-checked;
- Setting a reliable and experienced agent to study and check the
  person under scrutiny;
- Organizing surveillance or counter-surveillance on the person under scrutiny;
- Carrying out a secret search of his quarters;
- 'Recruiting' the target of study into another intelligence service
  with the help of the checking agent;
- Obtaining reliable data on the target of study by means of agents
  working in hostile Intelligence or Counter-Intelligence Services;
- The utilization of agent facilities to mount the operational-technical measures listed below.

III. Checking with the help of operational-technical methods

1. *Checking by means of postal correspondence*

- By sending to the address of the person under study a series of
  letters (a minimum of 5 or 6) from third countries and also from
  other cities in the country of residence;
- By putting test-letters directly into the post-box in the person's
  quarters or place of work with all the necessary stamps provided
  by the Centre together with various characteristics for detecting if
  it has been opened, including a chemical substance to detect the
  appearance of fingerprints on the enclosure;
- The object of study forwards his reports using test SW [secret writ-
  ing] copying paper (pseudo copy) treated specially for checking
  against a possible [hostile] chemical analysis with the object of establishing the composition of the SW including attempts to cut off
  small strips for such an analysis.

It is essential to adhere to the following operational-technical requirements in preparing test-letters:

– The form of the letter must exactly conform to the usage of the country in question (envelope, paper, style of address, quantity, type and value of postage stamps, correct lay-out etc);

– The open text must correspond to the operational cover story for the correspondence and the distinguishing marks on the envelope; it must be written and spelt correctly in whatever language is used. When doing the text of the letter, avoid the use of registered type-writers;

– in selecting an address for reply, it is more suitable to use actual and existing addresses where it is difficult to find the sender (institutes, schools, communal dwelling-houses, pensions, tourist centers etc);

– test-letters must not be kept longer than the period agreed with the 14th Department of the First Chief Directorate as in excess of this time the characteristics incorporated to detect unsealing will make it impossible to conduct a qualitative analysis.

2. *Checking by means of test containers and pockets*

This can be done by sending the person under study to the area for which a cover story has been prepared in order to receive or despatch test containers simulating the arrival (or despatch) of important intelligence material from or to a 'valuable source', using different left-luggage lockers (at airports, railway stations, bus stations etc).

In this case the operation itself may be carried out as follows:

a) the container is placed by a case officer, trusted agent or illegal and a receipt (or key) subsequently forwarded to the address of the person under examination so that the latter may withdraw the container and forward it to the case officer;

b) the container is placed by the case officer, trusted agent or illegal and the receipt (key) transmitted to the person being checked by means of DLB or by personal contact with the case officer (without previously notifying him of the location of the DLB or of the left-luggage locker);

c) the object of study is entrusted with a container to be placed
by him in a left-luggage locker and the receipt (key) in a
DLB which will subsequently be emptied by the object of
study himself or by the case officer under the pretext of a
'hitch' in the operation involving the arrival of a 'valuable
agent' to effect the despatch.

Another method of checking is the use of the residence (dacha, garage, office, etc) belonging to the person under examination for 'storing' test containers (packets) for fixed periods for supposed despatch to
'a valuable agent' who will come to collect the packet under previously
arranged conditions of contact. The operation permits of two variants:

a) the object of study returns the packets to the case officer on
the expiry of the stipulated period on the instructions of the
letter;
b) the packet is collected by another case officer or co-opted
person in the guise of a foreigner with due regard for essential security measures ensuring that the checking operation
is not blown if the person under study is in contact with
hostile special services.

The residence (dacha, place of work) of the object of study may
be used for the 'reception' of test containers (packets) from 'a valuable agent' in accordance with agreed contacting conditions and their
subsequent despatch to a case officer. The delivery of the container is
carried out by another case officer or co-opted person adopting the
necessary security measures to avoid blowing the checking operation
and to avoid the launching of provocation measures against us in the
event that the object of study is in contact with hostile special services.

The object of study can be despatched to an area (airports, railway
stations, seaports, restricted areas, other countries etc) for which a cover story has been prepared for a meeting with 'a valuable agent' in order to 'receive or despatch' test containers (packets) as outlined below:

a) the person under study goes for a meeting which is 'abort-
ed' for 'objective' reasons, with the subsequent return of the
container to the case officer;
b) a meeting is arranged between the object of study and
another case officer or co-opted person in the guise of a

foreigner; the necessary security precautions are observed in order to exclude the possibility of blowing the fact that it is a checking operation in case the object of study is in contact with hostile special services.

The object of study can be despatched to a cover area for which a cover-story has been prepared for the reception or despatch of test containers by means of a DLB as outlined below:

a)   The DLBs are filled by a case officer, trusted agent or illegal and cleared by the person under study at a pre-arranged signal (without his being informed in advance about the position of the DLB);

b)   The DLB is filled by the object of study but then the operation is subsequently cancelled due to the non-arrival of a 'valuable agent', with the container then being collected by the target himself or the case officer.

In the latter case it is essential to provide the person under study with a convincing cover-story to avoid revealing to him the fact that it is a test operation (in case of possible links between him and hostile special services).

When arranging verification measures using test containers (packets) one must bear in mind that these may be carried out with the help of a great diversity of special aids, chemical, photographic and mechanical, which permit a high degree of reliability in establishing whether a container has been opened, whether there has been contact with the contents, whether separate elements have been moved, checks made for SW, or enclosures substituted, whether there are fingerprints or the container and contents have been exposed to X-rays. As regards the last-named it must be borne in mind that special services are now equipped with special X-ray devices (to obtain an image by means of individual impulses) which do not involve exposing any films packed in the container or erasing any magnetically recorded messages.

Additionally when drawing up plans for, and putting into effect, this type of test operation the following operational requirements must be observed:

– The cover-story, the nature and choice of place where the check takes place must flow in a logical sequence from work previously undertaken with the target so as to convince him of the continuity of the proposed operational ploy;

– The containers used must, both with regard to their contents and the camouflage employed, fit into the cover-story;

– The verification operation itself must relate closely to agent-operational conditions and specific events, so as to convince the target of study and the special services (in a double-agent case) that the operation is a genuine operational one;

– The duration of the check must be planned in such a way that the special services (taking into account the technical and operational facilities at their disposal), would be able without under haste to unseal the container, study the contents and return it to its original condition;

– In order to obtain positive results in checking the target of study by means of this type of operation it is essential to think in terms of carrying out more than one (a minimum of five or six).

ON WAYS, METHODS AND DEVICES USED BY AGENTS OF WESTERN INTELLIGENCE SERVICES FOR THE COLLECTION OF INTELLIGENCE INFORMATION ON THE GSFG [GROUP OF SOVIET FORCES IN GERMANY] 2/D — 38 SS

THE ASPIRATIONS OF IMPERIALIST INTELLIGENCE SERVICE AS REGARDS THE GSFG

Special attention is given to obtaining information on the most important changes taking place in the armed forces, on signs of tension, as well as the absence of any such signs. The enemy attaches the greatest importance to information on the following:

1. Missile units.
2. Air Force and anti-aircraft units and formations.
3. Large railway junctions, railway stations used for loading and unloading of troops and equipment.
4. Branch lines running alongside military zones.
5. All kinds of tanks, artillery installations, special means of transport: tractors, including those without missiles; all special vehicles; generators, charging and compressor installations, radar stations, infra-red devices, and other things.

6. All newly built military complexes.
7. Firing ranges, bombing areas, river-crossing points.
8. All kinds of workshops for the repair of weapons and equipment.
9. Depots and stores for weapons, ammunition and food.
10. Main roads constantly being used by troops and which go to firing ranges and concentration areas.
11. Radio-relay networks and lines of the GSFG which are covered by the apparatus of an anti-aircraft system.
12. Lines of air-liaison going to military installations, location of cables, thickness and number of wires in a cable.

The recruiting attempts of enemy Intelligence Services vis-à-vis Soviet citizens which are aimed at military personnel:

1. Staff Officers.
2. Missile and radar personnel, and pilots.
3. Officers responsible for bringing the armed forces to a heightened state of battle readiness and those responsible for the supplying of units with ammunition.
4. Military doctors.
5. Soviet citizens who have contacts with local inhabitants.

Special attention is devoted to persons who are:

6. Dissatisfied with their jobs.
7. In the habits of over-indulging in alcoholic drinks.
8. In contact with German women.
9. Greedy for money.
10. Admirers of the Western way of life, greedy for material possessions. (All this being done with a view to intensifying these vices even further.)

The enemy also considers the following *factors to be conductive to recruitment:*

1. Critical attitude towards Soviet reality.
2. Excessive ambition.
3. Breakdown in family life or marriage.
4. Tendency to include in alcoholic drinks.

Individual Soviet Military personnel can come to the attention of the Western Special Intelligence Services:

1. As a result of contacts with foreigners in the territory of the USSR, before being posted to the GSFG, or while at home on leave.
2. From material based on questions put by repatriates, as well as private businessmen visiting the USSR or the GDR.
3. By publishing scientific or other articles in the open press.
4. As result of leads followed up by Intelligence organs.
5. By sending letters of a slanderous or anti-Soviet character to *Svoboda* [Freedom newspaper] and other publications.
6. Under influence of relatives or other contacts living in capitalist countries.
7. On the basis of *intimate relation with women* who are agents of foreign Intelligence Service.
8. As a result of marrying German women with relatives living in the West.
9. As a result of amoral behaviour, speculative deals, conspicuous peculiar behaviour, work missing operations and so on.
10. As a result of frequenting civilian [word missing] in East Berlin.

Places which may be used by enemy Intelligence Services for studying Soviet citizens for the purpose of eventual recruitment:

1. In establishments where official meetings take place between representatives of enemy Armed Forces and Soviet Military personnel.
2. In places where Soviet citizens meet with German commercial firms and/or other German organisations to arrange food and other supply questions.
3. During unofficial contacts and visits to taverns, restaurants, shops, cinemas.
4. Directly within Soviet military installations which have been penetrated by Western intelligence agencies, through Germans who are working there.
5. In Officers Club.
6. In buildings where Soviet Liaison Missions are located.
7. In places where international gathering take place (Leipzig Erfurt).
8. In Sanatoria (Bad Emster).

Attempts to recruit agents from amongst the local population are aimed at those:

1. Working in Soviet military institutions.
2. Residing in the vicinity of Soviet military installations.
3. Working in building-firms, motor-car repairs or other repair services.
4. Working at railway stations.
5. Connected with servicing Soviet citizens, e.g. tailor-shops.
6. Women of easy virtue or prostitutes.

Some revealing traits in the behaviour of enemy agents:

1. Regular visits to areas in the vicinity of Soviet military installations.
2. Regular journeys outside the confines of his usual place of residence.
3. Ascertaining that the suspected person dispatches mail posted in a place outside his place of residence.
4. Posting to West Germany of printed matter—newspapers not having a political bent.
5. Receiving letters from West Germany.
6. Finding on the suspected person town-maps printed by the firm Dewag (with a grid).
7. Establishing friendly relations with persons residing at military installations.
8. Journeys to Socialist countries (Yugoslavia, Cuba).
9. Posting letters to the following addresses in West Germany: BND, Baden-Wurtenberg, Halderberg, Mannheim; American and French Intelligence in West Berlin; Department for the Defence of the Constitution in West Berlin, Cologne, Aachen, Hamburg, Bonn, Wuppertal, Ragen.

Characteristic behavioural patterns in an agent engaged in visual observation:

1. General nervousness, constrained movements, frequent looking over one's shoulder.
2. Aim to leave quickly the place being observed.

3. Haste in showing documents justifying presence at a Soviet military installation.
4. Confused replies regarding the reason for presence at a Soviet military installation.

Some revealing traits in the actions of an agents receiving one-way transmissions or engaged in radio communications:

1. Keeping awake two nights running (at times of crisis, etc.).
2. Ascertaining the fact of postal correspondence being dispatched immediately after the day fixed for radio transmission.
3. Discovery of his definite frequencies, note-books with five-figure groups.
4. Presence in the attic, in his room or in a shed of large aerials erected for transmission, or of insulated pieces of wire which could be used as an aerial.
5. Use of headphones.
6. Creating the impression that the suspected person is absent from the flat at the time of reception.
7. Refusal to receive visitors especially on the days of reception.
8. Recording radio broadcasts on a tape-recorder.
9. Concealment of knowledge in radio matters.

Some instructions given by enemy Intelligence to their agents engaged in visual observation:

1. Not to allow any change to take place in either public or private way of life when beginning intelligence activities.
2. Conceal sympathy for Western way of life.
3. React calmly to all provocations from various people.
4. Not to establish contacts with obvious enemies of East Germany.
5. Before visiting the target to be observed, prepare cover story.
6. Go to the target to be observed accompanied by family.
7. Not to carry out observation always wearing the same clothes and to go there at various times of day.
8. Not to allow any notes to be made while in the area of the military installation.
9. Not to carry out observation during week-ends.
10. Visit the target on days of holiday (Red Army Day, May-Day, November).

11. For more prolonged observation of the target, make use of a non-working activity (sun-bathing, all sorts of walks).
12. Targets to which access is difficult are to be observed in the guise of mushroom-pickers, etc.
13. Make observations of firing ranges and training.
14. Visit Soviet troops and stores.
15. Make use of suitably-located windows of your flat.
16. Exposure of agents and illegal amongst specialist-military personal serving with NATO operating in areas surrounding military installations.

Established means of agents dispatch:

1. Under cover of returnees.
2. Going over to East Germany in the guise of deserters from the Bundeswehr [Armed Forces, FRG]
3. In the guise of sailors on West German ships, leaving the ship on arrival in an East German port.
4. Illegal crossed of the border.

Instructions given to "Rangers":

1. Not to do anything which would attract attention or give cause for investigating past background (not to enlist in the East German State Security Service, not to aim at rewards).
2. Behave in a loyal manner towards the GDR.

Give-away signs identifying an agent of enemy Intelligence, planted by the latter on our own Intelligence Agencies:

1. Too hasty investigation of West German authorities into agent's anti-Government attitudes.
2. Mention of relatives or friends working in various secret establishments.
3. Suggestions for a meeting by the agents which follow all rules of conspiracy or otherwise.
4. Target himself invites recruitment.
5. In writing down a message, target leaves a clear field at the top, without having first received instructions to do so, etc.
6. On being given a definite task, target finds it difficult to give an answer.
7. Target himself offering to do various things on own initiative.

Defection

Vladimir Kuzichkin was a career Soviet intelligence officer working in the First Directorate of the KGB, whose 1977–82 posting in Tehran looking after the Soviet Union's "illegals" in Iran spanned the transition from the rule of the Shah, through the Islamic Revolution of 1979 to the theocratic regime of Ayatollah Khomeini. There was little in his background to indicate he was a potential defector, but the memoir he subsequently wrote (*Inside the KGB*) documents his gradual disillusionment with the corruption and careerism in the communist party that was both strangling the Soviet Union and hampering the efficient operation of its intelligence services. It was not a comfortable time to be a Soviet diplomat in Iran, let alone a KGB operative. In the first part of his tenure, Kuzichkin faced the hostility of the Shah's distinctly pro-American Savak secret police and then the turmoil of the 1979 revolution and the installation of the Khomeini regime. The new Islamist government viewed the Soviet Union with distinct suspicion, especially in view of its previous sponsorship of the Tudeh, the Iranian Communist Party, which was marginalized following the Revolution. The Tudeh was then subject to a programme of mass arrest in 1982, making Soviet intelligence operations in Iran even more perilous. In April that year Kuzichkin found that a cache of secret documents concerning illegals that he had hidden in the embassy in case of attempts to storm it by Iranian revolutionaries had been opened and the contents stolen. As the penalty for losing secret material was seven years imprisonment, he decided he had no choice but to defect. Using all his expertise in providing documentation for illegal agents, he travelled to Tabriz on his Soviet diplomatic passport and then, having navigated several checkpoints manned by the feared Revolutionary Guards, used a foreign passport to cross into Turkey. He made contact with British intelligence and ended up living in the United Kingdom. The details of Soviet agents in Iran which he provided to MI6 were allegedly later leaked back to the Iranians, allowing their arrest and the severe disruption of KGB activities in the country.

EXTRACT FROM *INSIDE THE KGB*: 'WHAT WOULD COMRADE LENIN HAVE DONE?'

Chapter 20

By the beginning of 1982 the Soviet Union had decided on its policy towards the Iran–Iraq war. This policy favoured Iraq, which the
Soviet Union began overtly to supply with arms, while showing itself
increasingly contemptuous towards Iran. On several occasions the
Soviet air force made raids on Iranian territory from Afghanistan,
in order to strike at camps where Afghan partisans were undergoing
training. No one fell over backwards to apologize.

It was obvious by now that as a result of the policies it had been
pursuing, Iran had virtually isolated itself from the rest of the world.
So long as Khomeini was alive, Iran would never return to the
American fold. That was the prospect which had worried the Soviet
rulers most of all. The Soviet Union was far better off with an Iran
that was weak and stewing in its own juice. From the Soviet Union's
standpoint, Iran was no longer an important country. This also found
expression in the appointment of the new ambassador to Tehran.
Vinogradov had been a member of the Party's Central Committee;
Boldyrev, the new ambassador, had held the very modest position of
head of the Middle East Department in the Soviet foreign ministry.
Vinogradov left Iran in the spring of 1982, and he was given some
high ceremonial post in the governing establishment.

Oddly enough, and much to our surprise, Iran reacted to the
cooling Soviet attitude in an almost placatory way. The Iranian authorities grew less truculent. The press adopted a softer tone towards
the Soviet Union. The slogan 'Death to the Soviet Union' was almost
dropped. Furthermore, the Iranian–Soviet negotiations on economic
cooperation were renewed on the Iranians' initiative. A new treaty on
the further development of economic cooperation between Iran and
the Soviet Union was signed in Moscow in February 1982. Soviet
specialists began to return to Iran.

Against that background, the conditions around the Soviet embassy began to return to normal. Anti-Soviet Afghan demonstrators
went on parading in Tehran, but this time we were very well protected.
On the next anniversary of the Afghan revolution in April 1982, the

demonstrators were not even allowed near the embassy, which was ringed by a remarkably large number of police and Revolutionary Guards. The Iranians were now afraid that something might happen to us, and were doing everything possible to carry out their promise, given earlier in Moscow, to guarantee the safety of Soviet citizens.

In these circumstances I decided that there was no longer any point in keeping the film of secret documents in the cache, and that it should now be taken out and destroyed. I went into the Impulse station premises during the lunch-break, when no one was there, and went to the cache. Then I squatted down and began to prise at the skirting board. To my surprise, it fell away from the wall at the first touch. That is a part of it fell off, near where the cache was. Under the skirting board gaped an empty hole. The container and the film had disappeared. I could not believe my eyes and checked everything again, but with the same result. The cache was empty. Only then did I realize that the skirting board had not been fixed tightly in place, as we had left it when we filled the cache, but had only been leaning against the wall. Whoever had removed the film in haste had not had time to stick the skirting board back.

I sat there in a state of shock still squatting, and stared long and hard at the empty opening in the wall. For me, this empty space was a tragedy. It was the end of the road. Under Soviet law, seven years in jail is the minimum sentence for losing top-secret documents. Whoever stole the film must have known this. In a mean, low-down way, in the Soviet way, someone had dealt me a fatal stab in the back. As to who it could have been, I could only guess. Officially, only Resident Shebarshin knew of the cache besides myself. Whom else he could have told about it, I did not know. But that no longer mattered. Whoever did it had created an irreversible situation. He could not put the film back in the cache, or, let us say, give it surreptitiously to the resident. That would be a clear indication that I had nothing to do with it. He could only destroy the film and sit and wait until its loss was officially discovered. In any event the responsibility for the loss of these top-secret documents lay on my shoulders.

My brilliant career was over. And that career had indeed been brilliant. I had been promoted three times in military rank, rising from lieutenant to major in the course of only one tour of duty in Iran. But more important than rank was promotion in the posts I held. In these too I was promoted three times during my tour of duty. From junior case officer I rose through the posts of case officer and senior case officer to that of assistant head of department. In addition, I had been given to understand unofficially in the Centre that my candidature was being seriously considered for the post of head of a geographical section after I had finally returned from Iran. In the KGB, such quick promotion in the course of only five years' service does not happen often. Now everything had come crashing down. And not only that. It was the ruin of all my secret plans for what I intended to do after I got back to the Soviet Union.

My first impulse was to go to the resident immediately and tell him everything, and then to find and punish the rat who had done it. But I realized that this would lead nowhere and would amount to virtual suicide. The resident would have to report it to the Centre, whose only possible response would be to recall me to Moscow for an inquiry. I decided to wait before reporting.

At that moment Arkadi Glazyrin, the Impulse station operator, returned from his lunch-break. When he saw me sitting there at the wall, he asked me what I was doing. I gave him the straight answer that I had opened my cache and had not found what should have been inside, but added that its contents were not too important. Arkadi inspected the empty cache, dug around inside it with his hand, and then, after muttering something, went off into his room. He cannot have attached any great importance to it. It was just as well that he did not.

I was in a strange state in the days that followed. I was one person who went to work, wrote telegrams to the Centre, and talked to my friends. At the same time I was another person who could think constantly of one thing only – WHAT CAN I DO? I could not eat. My body refused food. At night I was tortured by nightmares, or rather always by the same dream – a man dressed all in black, with an axe raised over his head, approaches my bed to finish me off. At that point I awoke in terror.

What could I do, I thought. Report it, or equally, sit and wait until it was discovered and then begin to prove my innocence? But that was no use. In my country, those who stumble and fall are trampled to death. To scorn danger and proudly take your punishment, while you fight on to prove your innocence, means adding your name to the list of the millions of victims of the Soviet system. And for the sake of what? For I already hated all that with all my heart. Nobody would appreciate my sacrifice, nobody needed it, and what did I have to prove to a system I despised?

'What would Comrade Lenin have done in your place?' I suddenly recalled the comical question often asked by the positive heroes of Soviet literature. All right, I thought, what would he have done? 'He would have emigrated,' were the words that sounded lucidly and clearly in my head. It seemed to me at that moment that it was not really my response, but that somebody else had said it. No, I thought. That's not for me. I had never been pro-Western. I always thought that the West had its own interests, and that it needed a strong Russia like a hole in the head, whether it was a communist Russia or a free Russia. I believed that we, the Russians, had to solve our own problems, and that changes in the Soviet structure were possible only from within, and absolutely not from outside. Interference from outside would as always unite the people and only strengthen the regime.

But the more I thought about this, the more I came to the conclusion that I had no other way out, no matter how I might try to avoid it. And in the West I should be able in some way or other to realize my plans. The thought again occurred that most of the Bolshevik leaders, who knew a thing or two about resistance, had spent a great part of their pre-revolutionary lives as emigrants abroad, and derived only advantage from it. What about Russia? I asked myself, for Russia does not like traitors. But the Russia that I was trying to serve, living on a diet of illusions, existed only in my head. The fact is that what has existed in Russia from the moment the Bolsheviks took power is hostile to her, and to fight it is the sacred duty of all Russians. So why waver now? That is what was going through my head at the time.

My nervous tension was so great that I began to take to the bottle to get rid of it. That helped. Then one evening I happened to run into Mylnikov, our Party leader. We met in the embassy grounds. He was drunk as usual, and when he saw me he invited me round to his flat to sink some more. I did not like the man, and it was never my habit to drink with his kind, but that evening something impelled me and I agreed. After a couple of drinks in Mylnikov's flat we had an argument, and at that point my dam burst. I told Mylnikov everything I thought about the Party, communism, the KGB, everything. For me at that moment, Mylnikov was the embodiment of everything I hated. That encounter would have ended fatally for Mylnikov had Levakov the security officer not arrived at the flat. The neighbours had complained about the racket from Mylnikov's flat. It turned out that Mylnikov had already had two rows with other people that day before he met me.

Levakov was surprised when he saw me, and said that he never expected that I might keep such company. 'I didn't expect it either,' I answered him. But it had happened, and a good many neighbours must have overheard our conversation. Sound carried far in the embassy block of flats. It was like talking face to face with everybody. I was certain that I would be reminded in due course of my candid revelations.

One day in a private conversation, one of our cipher clerks told me what he thought was a funny story. Friends in the Centre had told him that the commission that oversees the security systems for storing KGB documents had visited embassies in several Latin American countries and had found so many security breaches that it had now been decided to screen all Soviet embassies abroad. The cipher clerk said that it would be our turn soon, but there was nothing for him to worry about – he had all his records completely in order. If his story appeared funny to him, I for my part saw little in it to laugh about. The loss of my documents could be discovered even before the commission arrived, for our cipher clerks would begin their own check before the appearance of the commission. When I asked him when the commission was due, he replied that he didn't yet know exactly, but they were planning to come in the summer.

I had to act at once, since the preparations for my move could take a great deal of time. The first thing to decide was which route I should take to leave Iran. Of the existing passport check-points on the Iranian frontier, those on the Soviet, Afghan, Pakistani and Iraqi borders were out for a start. That left only Mehrabad airport in Tehran and the Bazargan check-point on the Turkish–Iranian frontier.

It would have been tempting of course to board an aircraft and fly off from Iran to the other end of the world. But there were serious objections to my using Mehrabad airport. First, practically everyone there had known me for several years, as I appeared there about once a week. Second, there were always many Soviet nationals knocking about in the airport. This meant that, if the airport were chosen, it would only be possible to fly out on my personal Soviet passport. Even buying the tickets on that passport would be very risky, as it would be noticed. It does not happen often in Iran that a Soviet official flies off to Europe on his own. But were it to happen, news about it could reach the Aeroflot representative. And it would have been quite stupid for me to use a foreign passport in Mehrabad airport, since everybody there knew me.

My work with illegals taught me to think out everything, down to the last detail, and to pre-empt all possible contingencies. Mistakes lead to failures. In my case, they would have led to catastrophe. There was only one way left – Bazargan, the check-point on the Turkish–Iranian frontier. The unfavourable factor here was that Bazargan was 900 kilometers from Tehran. In other respects, nothing could have been better. I had a solid reason to give to the Iranians for making a trip to the north-west. There were Soviet specialists in Tabriz, which is no more than 200 kilometers from Bazargan, and as a consular official I had the right to make a trip into that area. Also, I knew the procedures at the Bazargan check-point very well, as it was part of my duties to gather information of this nature. So that was to be the crossing point.

Now for the documents. Unfortunately I could not use a Soviet passport. Had it been an official journey, the Iranian foreign ministry would have given prior notification to the local authorities that a Soviet diplomat would appear at the Bazargan check-point. That meant that I should have to provide myself with a foreign passport. Here I had to summon up all the knowledge I had accumulated as an officer of the documentation department of illegal intelligence. I obtained the passport.

In order to travel through Iran, a foreigner must hold a permit issued by the Iranian foreign ministry. I decided to travel on my Soviet diplomatic documents from Tehran as far as Tabriz, and I had no great difficulty in having a permit for the journey made out in the Iranian foreign ministry without anyone in our consulate knowing anything about it.

While I was in the process of preparing all the details of the plan, I was completely composed. I knew that the decision I had taken was the only right one. Not once did I have even the slightest niggle of a doubt. I simply kept constantly recalling some lines of a Vysotsky poem;

> Pure Truth will surely triumph
> If it does the same
> As blatant Falsehood.

This poem takes the form of an allegory relating how Truth was robbed by Falsehood (an allusion to the 1917 revolution). Falsehood did that in order to triumph. Now Truth must do the same.

It took me some time to make my preparations, but finally they were completed. Everything was ready. All that remained was to pick the day. In the end, it fixed itself. I knew that Levakov had been planning for months to make an inspection trip to the Soviet–Iranian border with Turkmenistan. There was a check-point there for travellers crossing from Iran to the Soviet Union and back, and there was nothing out of the ordinary in the embassy security officer planning to visit it. But now he was insisting that I should accompany him, and this put me on my guard. Perhaps there was nothing behind it. I do not know. But it would have been stupid to run the risk. What was more, Levakov was planning to cross over on to Soviet territory, just for familiarization purposes, and then come back. I did not like that at all.

In any case, even if I were mistaken in my thinking, it did not matter. The longer I stayed, the worse my chances grew. Of course I agreed to Levakov's proposal about the trip, and we fixed it for 18 June 1982. I also offered to draw up all the travel documents. My own departure would have to take place before then.

The day of my departure fell on Wednesday, 2 June 1982, in the evening. I spent that entire day as usual in the embassy, doing the usual things in the consular department in the morning before going on to the Residency. Once again I checked everything in my office, to be sure I had left no traces of what I had been doing with the documents. I had left my car outside the embassy grounds the previous day, but I told people that I had left it in a garage in town for servicing. The same day I visited the accounts desk in the Residency, in order to pay off what I owed. I did not want to be accused of peculation on top of everything else. After lunch I spent my allotted time in the Impulse station, following the Iranians' radio conversations. This enabled me to acquaint myself with the operational conditions in town that day. I then went back to my flat, checked everything again, and put it all in order.

At 6 o'clock in the evening I left the flat for the last time. I decided to leave the embassy by going through the quiet economic section, instead of through our guards' office, where all comings and goings were recorded. In the guards' office of the economic section, on the other hand, no one paid any attention to KGB officers who passed through it on their way out. And they knew me already. All I was carrying was a plastic bag, in which I had put my jacket and tie. It would have been unnatural to go out wearing them, as the weather was so hot.

On the way to the guards' office I bumped into a Residency officer who worked in the economic section, and he asked where I was going. To the dry cleaners, I replied. He was not really interested and hastened off on his own affairs. Once beyond embassy territory, I went to where I had parked the car. What if it wasn't there? The question crossed my mind. What if it had been stolen? But the car was there where I had left it.

I still had one more thing to do, and that was to carry out surveillance detection procedures. The Iranian security service could not be allowed to put their finger on my very last operation. On the detection route I could see no surveillance in my rear mirror. After checking thoroughly for two hours I was satisfied that I was not being tailed and decided to stop weaving through the town. As it was 8 o'clock in the evening, still too soon to leave Tehran, I decided to go to a quiet restaurant in the Abbasabad quarter and have a meal before setting out on my long journey, but I had no appetite. My nervous tension had begun to tell. Still, I made myself eat a shashlyk and drink some water. By then it was 9 o'clock, and darkness was beginning to fall on Tehran. The time had come. I nosed my car out of the narrow sidestreets and, no longer checking for surveillance, drove off towards the west.

The way out from town lay through Shahyad Square, one end of which was then guarded by soldiers and Revolutionary Guards. There a soldier armed with a rifle signalled me to stop and demanded to see my travel documents. I produced them. The soldier read through them unhurriedly.

'Odd,' he said. 'A Soviet diplomat driving westwards?'

'I'm going to Tabriz on embassy business,' I answered calmly. 'What's odd about that?'

The soldier was about to say something else, but just at that moment a large bus drove up from behind, and all the guards rushed to search it. They also called the soldier. He handed back my documents and waved me on. The danger had passed. I put my foot down on the accelerator, and my BMW disappeared into the darkness, leaving Tehran behind for ever.

It was a real pitch-black southern night, and I only saw what was picked up by my headlights. The excellent road ran in a north-westerly direction. Thanks to the French, who built it, I was making a fair speed, and about one hour later I passed through Qazvin, almost 140 kilometres from Tehran. I did not stop, for I had to pass through Tabriz as early in the morning as I could, in case some casual Soviet specialist should chance to see my car with its embassy number-plates.

After I had left Qazvin behind, I suddenly saw flashing lights in my mirror, approaching from the rear. It turned out to be a traffic police car. I slowed down. They caught up, and drove alongside for a time, inspecting me. I looked back at them. A moment later the police car accelerated and shot forward, its lights still flashing. What does that mean, I thought. Have they rumbled me, or was it just curiosity? But that was no longer important. I just had to press on ahead.

As I approached the town of Mianeh, I felt myself beginning to tire. My eyes were closing. I saw an illuminated parking area, and pulled into it. A small shop was open and I bought some water. I tried to take a nap for about fifteen minutes, but sleep did not come and I decided to continue my journey. It was 5 o'clock in the morning when I passed through Tabriz, which was still deserted. Just beyond the town, I found myself having to fight to stay awake, in fact at one point I realized that I had dozed off only when the car wheels hit the edge of the road. I could not take this risk any more, so I pulled over and fell asleep at once.

Instead of the fifteen minutes I had allowed myself, I slept for forty. This was a loss which I could not make up, but I floored the accelerator and drove on. I just had to arrive at the Bazargan checkpoint no later than 9 o'clock, by the time the frontier opened. After that hour, the main cross-border traffic began – huge lorries on their way through Turkey and beyond to Europe – and ordinary mortals could not pass. If I failed to cross the frontier on Thursday, I should have to wait until Saturday, for Friday was a holiday when the check-point was closed. I could not let this happen, since by then my absence from the embassy would have been discovered and the alarm raised.

Keyed up with speed and urgency, I reached Bazargan at 8.45 a.m. The road to the check-point, straight as an arrow, was full of lorries, which stretched in line for about a kilometre. I stopped the car, gathered up all my Soviet documents and hid them thoroughly inside it. Then with my foreign passport ready, I drove up to the gates that led into the frontier zone. The fairly sleepy civilian orderly on duty only glanced at my passport and let me through. Now I had to leave the car. I drove it into a parking area full of lorries, washed myself with what was left of the water, and put on my jacket and tie. The suitcase with my personal things was in the boot. I took it out, locked the car, and walked off towards the check-point.

The parking area where I had left the car lay in a hollow, and I had to stumble my way up a steep embankment. Reaching the top, I ran straight into a group of armed Revolutionary Guards, who were just walking past at that moment. They stopped right in front of me.

'Who are you?' one of them asked, speaking Farsi.

I answered in English that I did not understand. Then another of them, who looked fairly respectable for a Guard, asked the same question in English. I had begun to explain that I was going to Turkey, when it dawned on me that my listeners were becoming increasingly wide-eyed in astonishment. What was this? Suddenly I realized that, without having the foggiest idea I was doing so because of my nervousness, I had begun to explain myself in pure Farsi.

'Ah, so you do speak Farsi,' said the first Guard.

'Yes, but very little,' I answered in English again. That did not satisfy them.

'How did you get here?'

I explained that I had been brought by a friend, who had already gone back.

'Let's go and ask the duty orderly at the gates,' said the first Guard, unconvinced.

Everything inside me seized up. I preferred not to think what would happen now, as we walked back towards the gates. One Guard kept my passport, the other carried my suitcase. The sleepy duty orderly was getting ready to check the lorries. We went up to him.

'This is the end of my adventure,' I thought.

'Do you remember this gentleman?' the Guard asked the orderly, pointing at me.

The orderly nodded.

'How did he get here?'

It was obvious that the orderly was extremely frightened. He probably thought that the Guards wanted to pin something on him.

'By car,' the orderly answered.

'How many people were in the car?' the Guard continued, interrogating the orderly, with his eyes fixed penetratingly upon him.

At this point, without knowing how I did it, I whispered to myself under my breath in Farsi, 'Two, and the car has already gone back.'

'Two,' replied the orderly. 'And the car has already gone back.' I could not believe my ears!

'Ah,' said the Guard turning to me, 'that means that you told the truth. May I offer our apologies for detaining you. Here are your passport and things. We'll give you a lift, as it's rather a long walk to the check-point'

They called up a light vehicle, and the driver drove me straight to the check-point building. I did not say another word so as not to betray my nervousness.

Another surprise lay in wait at the check-point. Under the new rules, every foreigner who crossed the frontier had to be interviewed by a representative of the Iranian security service. Out of the frying pan into the fire. I was taken into a side room. At a desk sat, certainly not a former SAVAK official, but a bearded, scruffy-looking youth. I was in luck, for he spoke no English. An officer from passport control translated our conversation. I sat and looked the bearded one straight in the face, but his eyes were shifty. He asked what I had been doing in Iran.

'Business,' I answered curtly.

'And what do you think of Reagan and Margaret Thatcher?' he asked, looking somewhere to one side.

'Politics don't interest me, and I don't intend to discuss these matters with someone like you,' I answered impertinently.

The officer who was interpreting gave me a startled look and began to translate what I had said in considerably softer tones. But the bearded one had correctly understood my tone. He began to bustle about, and quickly handed my passport to the officer, who leafed through the pages and said that everything was in order. His colleague waved towards the door with his hand, allowing me to leave. There was a large black telephone on the bearded one's desk. Throughout the interview I kept thinking uneasily that it might ring, and that he would be told where I had just come from, and that they had discovered my car. The ring never came.

Out in the corridor, the officer smiled apologetically, heaved a long-suffering sigh and handed back my passport. He led me to the doors of the customs hall. They were still locked, and the man with the keys did not appear for some five minutes that seemed like an eternity. Finally he arrived, but then could not find the one he needed as he sorted through the enormous bunch of keys he was carrying. Everything seemed to be moving at a pace more leisurely than in a slow-motion film.

At last the door was opened, and I passed into the customs hall. In the middle was an enormous circular counter, one side belonging to Iran, the other to Turkey. Another Revolutionary Guard-cum-customs man examined my suitcase, and then, quite unhurriedly, I walked round the counter and found myself on Turkish territory. Probably on purpose to annoy the Iranians, the Turks had opened a duty-free shop on their side of the hall which sold liquor. Hardly anyone checked me on the Turkish side, except that they looked long and hard at the photograph in the passport.

When I came out of the Turkish customs building, I looked back and saw beyond the barrier the bustling guards of the Islamic revolution. Now all this was well and truly behind me. To the right rose the proud towering beauty of Mount Ararat, that ancient spiritual symbol of the Armenian people. It passed into Turkish ownership after the 1917 revolution as a consequence of the policies of the Bolsheviks. And the thought crossed my mind that, like Mount Ararat, I was with the Motherland in spirit, but in body I was now in a foreign land.

CODE AND CIPHER-BREAKING CHALLENGE

Here are 16 codes and ciphers. They are broadly in increasing difficulty starting with a straightforward Caesar shift, followed by some forms of substitution cipher, then tracing the evolution of cryptography up until the Cold War period. Some are famous examples of enciphered texts from literature and history, although most have been constructed for this contest. The contest includes a wide variety of traditional codes and ciphers. You may (or may not) encounter codes based on Braille, Morse code (and fractionated Morse), semaphore, the NATO Phonetic alphabet, and computer codes, and other traditional and modern ciphers. Good Luck!

You have the chance to enter a challenge made up of two parts via the Pool of London Press website (www.pooloflondon.com). If you can decipher any five of the codes set out below, then you can enter the first contest. This should be achievable by many entrants. A random draw of all valid entrants will take place on 31 March 2016 and there will be five winners. The second contest will be won by a random draw of all entrants who get the most ciphers solved and there will be two winners. It will take place on the same day. The contest winners shall receive books of their choice to a certain value from the Pool of London Press, Casemate and related group companies. Please visit the Pool of London Press website for full competition rules, details of prizes and full Terms & Conditions. Correspondence will not be entered into.

The Publishers would like to thank Micheal Colao who has devised and set this code challenge.

1. JR XARJ JR JRER GNYXVAT NOBHG FCVRF.V XARJ
    UR XARJ V XARJ. V JNF QVTTVAT ZL BJA TENIR. –
    PUEVFGVAR XRRYRE

2. 53++!305))6★;4826)4+.)4+);806★;48!8`60))85;;]8★;:+★8
    !83(88)5★   !;46(;88★96★?;8)★+(;485);5★!2:★+(;4956★2(5★-
    4)8`8★;4069285);) 6!8)4++;1(+9;48081;8:8+1;48!85;4)485!528
    806★81(+9;48;(88;4(+? 34;48)4++;161;:188;+?;

3. jjfqhmbbnIagtbimtbP –
    .wfhtqtbgfbspmxwmeisrebmymxmlfjeisrebmym
    xmjfjXimjthNmajhtihf,ekxfbspmxwmeisrebmymxmlfjeisrebm
    ymftxxnB
    htjfajxtxmjfjXimjthNmajihfftxxnBhmmzjmrmghmbmpptix'efisJ

4. ∇⊓◻◻◻∨ЕϜϜϜЕ∨∨Lⵦ⨳◻,>⊓◻◁Lⵦ⨳◻◻ⵦ>∨
    Γ◻˥Ⴑ◻∨˥Γ◻∨,∪<>Γ◻ ∪⌐>>⌐Ⴑ˥Γ◻∨.-∇
    Γ˥Ⴑ˥Γ⌐⨳∨⊓⌐∪◻∨˥◻⌐Ϝ◻

5. AH-NAH A-KEH-DI-GLINI AH-JAH GAH TSAH-AS-ZIH
    BE-TKAH TSIN-TLITI TSE-NILL A-CHIN BE-TKAH
    TKIN KLESH BE-TKAH DIBEH SHI-DA GAH DAH-
    NES-TSA A-KHA SHI-DA TSAH CHINDI AH-NAH BE
    BE-TKAH BE-GHA BE-TKAH WOL-LA-CHEE BE-TKAH
    A-CHIN AH-JAH A-CHI KLIZZIE LIN SHUSH NE-AHS-
    JAH SHI-DA DAH-NES-TSA CHA TLO-CHIN NE-AHS-
    JAH CHINDI BE-TKAH TOH-NI-TKAL-LO BE-TKAH
    A-KEH-DI-GLINI NE-AHS-JAH DIBEH-YAZZIE SHI-DA
    TSAH THAN-ZIE WOL-LA-CHEE DAH-NES-TSA TSAH-
    AS-ZIH BE-TKAH DIBEH CLA-GI-AIH TKIN AH-NAH
    KLESH BE-TKAH BE-TKAH TKELE-CHO-G WOL-LA-
    CHEE TSAH DZEH BE-TKAH TSE-NILL SHI-DA DIBEH
    THAN-ZIE AH-NAH A-CHIN

6. 11:52, 22:37, 4:37, 00:37; 1:30, 21:15, 23:52; 19:30, 10:37, 1:37,
    22:45, 9:15, 16:45, 9:52; 19:07, 18:00, 19:52, 13:30, 2:45, 21:22,
    9:00, 14:52

7. kimono, gingivitis, inscription, strings, victimhood, indoor, big-
    foot, microbiotic, tricks, disproportion, microbiology, idiotic,
    flights, crippling, criminology, violins, thrills, Filipino, widow-
    hood, sight, spittoon, sigmoidoscopy, nincompoop, mirroring,
    Vikings, mitochondrion, idiomorphic, micro-zoology, socio-
    biology, digitising, incision, criminologist, Illinois, iconology,
    civilising, histrionics, jingoists, Microsoft Windows

8. þ ᴜᏻႹ₥ᴏⴕ ᖫ⌐ ᴄ\ʌᵐ ɣᵐĉℙ ɣííċ ℙċ૧íᵐ : λɣᵐ ǵ ℴ̇ṗ ᖫᴎᖕ
   þ λℴ̇ṗɣ̂ᴊ ᖫ ᴜᴎ ᖫ ɣᴚ ℙᵖ þ ɣṗᵐ₥ ᖫ ૧ᴚ ɜ̇ ℴíí₥ ᖫ⌐ þ λ₣̂ℙ̂ᴊ : ~

9. We are interested in the following six facts about flags (read left
   to right, top to bottom): Whether there is any red on the flag?,
   Whether there is at least one star on the flag (including the sun)?,
   Whether the flag uses exactly three colours?, Whether the Flag
   is for a European entity (including European dependencies)?,
   Whether there is any yellow on the flag, and for the purposes of
   this, a dark gold is not yellow?, and Whether the flag is that of
   an entity which is not a member state of the United Nations?
   – Burkina Faso, Andorra, Nauru, Switzerland, Sudan, Rwanda,
   Bangladesh, Panama, Belgium, Marshall Islands, Albania, The
   Former Yugoslav Republic of Macedonia, Azerbaijan, Kosovo,
   Spain, Romania, Brunei Darussalam, Afghanistan, Uruguay,
   Canada, Argentina, Cameroon, The Azores

10.
BVAEQ	CDWTP	MGZLB	ZSCPK	IMPSI	PVESG
VBMLO	BHWQP	TGVVX	PUMEY	WGJBT	HUPUY
EOWCG	MGAPP	BTTYI	RFPTH	LPSQS	HQWZJ
XMMXP	QIVNF	TJXCM	TOYHS	QRIRA	FKZOQ
EPZLU	MGPIW	SCAHB	TPLHO	QAXGI	OWFSC
BWTZZ	CGHVO	QCGOI	ATUXA	PZVPB	HZCJY
VLRZI	LALKL	SPT

[Hint. The key is 6 letters long]

11.
EBNOT	NEAFH	TEGTE	ANEHH	LTEEU	DEFAM
RRFMA	IROEN	CIRRS	HBTIP	ALHCY	MYAAI
EPDNN	SENET	XRESE	XTVPR	XIEIM	XNROS

12.
GXTEA	POTAQ	TSREH	EOROL	NQLLR
EHBOQ	VCHIF	OOFTA	RBHGD	CQTWV
VDUHX	KSTSW	STUNU	DORAK	SWSQR
KEASI	PITPR	ZPCQI	GC

13.
WLJIU	JYBRK	PWFPF	IJQSK	PWRSS	WEPTM
MJRBS	BJIRA	BASPP	IHBGP	RWMWQ	SOPSV
PPIMJ	BISUF	WIFOT	HWBIS	WBIQW	FBJRB
GPILP	PXLPM	SAJQQ	PMJQS	RJASW	LSBLW
GBHMJ	QSWIL	PXWOL

14. DK TH LH CK IG VT IZ PR KP RI SX AH
    RU OM RU IP NK LQ HU SY OM LQ GO SY
    OM KQ OM RU AG KP UT UQ GP CL QD VP
    PK RG RK RU VB RI SK WK LG GK AQ VO
    UZ RB MA RZ

15. RYULS   PRRAQ   LHCUL   ULNRS   LHGJV   NSUJR
    VNERF   PRSSD   QFPVR   FUQAN   TTSHO   VRISI
    WGVSS   BINWG   VJYPR   ANTTV   RFNBR   BOSHD
    UPWRF   TTHFN   JGPNE   SUJJR   GNUNP   REJWF
    NLSRV   BGWEB   YWGVP   BDSHJ   CNPUR   EYUJB
    E

16. M@PIS   M^QGQ   T_^W_   NM@]R   WO]]G   KH[KM
    PI\BX   [ATZU   JMGG[NIR^Q   LGZXG   IUCBU
    FEXGF   IYOGW   JG\@C   M@SIU   LKCAS   G@S\Q
    FIGGW   IFZ[V   G^AJA   SYP]Z   GZ\\S   KB\O\
    C@Y\]   ADT\P   QCGIQ   UEYB]   CAXKX   TEYBQ
    KZTG_   WGZZ[EYGGP   eMD[]   LC}EZ   M[[OG
    VC^W[PCFK}   EIZ\S   GGZXU   NFZFZ   CBAF[
    LUBOX   IIGGX   KMOLU   XHTGS   M^RAA   XI[E[
    JIGCU   LBRØF   VVGOX   RDXMS   GDPKS   GCGIQ
    @@TEQ

SOURCES

Chapter 1

Digest of Ham

Camp 020: *MI5 and the Nazi Spies: the official history of MI5's wartime interrogation centre* (introduced and edited by Oliver Hoare) Public Record Office, Richmond Surrey 2000

Mulholland Manual

The Official CIA Manual of Trickery and Deception (H Keith Melton and Robert Wallace)
HarperCollins, New York, 2010

Prikhodko Lecture

The Penkovsky Papers (Oleg Penkovsky, introduction and commentary by Frank Gibney, translated by Peter Deriabin) HarperCollins, London, 1965

Chapter 2

Suvorov on the Undercover Residency

Soviet Military Intelligence (Viktor Suvorov) Hamish Hamilton, London, 1984

Chapter 3

Vassiliev notebooks

"Vassiliev Yellow Notebook #1," 2009, History and Public Policy Program Digital Archive, Alexander Vassiliev Papers, Manuscript Division, Library of Congress.
http://digitalarchive.wilsoncenter.org/document/112856
and
"Vassiliev Yellow Notebook #2," 2009, History and Public Policy Program Digital Archive, Alexander Vassiliev Papers, Manuscript Division, Library of Congress.
http://digitalarchive.wilsoncenter.org/document/112857

Penkovsky Operation Plan

Taken from:
http://www.foia.cia.gov/sites/default/files/document_conversions/89801/DOC_0000012390.pdf

Chapter 4

Protocol M

The Soviet Secret Services (Otto Heilbrunn) Allen & Unwin, London 1956

Soviet Plan to Discredit Dulles

"Note from KGB Chairman A. Shelepin to Central Committee of the Communist Party of the Soviet Union, Regarding Plan to

Discredit CIA Chief Dulles," June 07, 1960, History and Public Policy Program Digital Archive, Shelepin to CC CPSU, TsKhSD, fond 4,
opis 13, delo 65, ll. 12–37 in Special Dossier of the Secretariat of the
Central Committee 153/30c from 14.VI.60 (14 June 1960).
http://digitalarchive.wilsoncenter.org/document/115975

Chapter 5

Stasi assessment of western intelligence techniques

"East German Ministry of State Security, 'New Methods of Operation of Western Secret Services'," November, 1958, History and
Public Policy Program Digital Archive, BStU, ZA, MfS-HA IX Nr.
4350, pp. 341–360. Translated by Paul Maddrell. Names redacted in
accordance with the German Law on State Security Records.
http://digitalarchive.wilsoncenter.org/document/118653

The East Germans/Russians discover a Western wire-tap tunnel extending into East Berlin

https://www.cia.gov/library/center-for-the-study-of-intelligence/
csi-publications/books-and-monographs/on-the-front-lines-
of-the-cold-war-documents-on-the-intelligence-war-in-berlin-
1946-to-1961/5-4.pdf

KGB assessment of nuclear war preparations/Operation Ryan

*Instructions from the Centre: Top Secret Files on KGB Foreign Operations
1975-85* (Christopher Andrew and Oleg Gordievsky) Hodder &
Stoughton, London 1993

Chapter 6

KGB Instructions for Checking Agents

*Instructions from the Centre: Top Secret Files on KGB Foreign Operations
1975-85* (Christopher Andrew and Oleg Gordievsky) Hodder &
Stoughton, London 1993

Vladimir Kuzichkin Defection

Inside the KGB: myth and reality (Vladimir Kuzichkin, translated
Thomas Beattie) London André Deutsch, 1990

DISGUISE KIT

The ability to hide "in clear sight" was essential for agents. This disguise kit, concealed in a standard men's toiletry bag, contained a variety of aids for an agent to modify his appearance. These include fake moustaches (for those who lacked them) and shaving gear (for those who wanted to remove them). There were also rubber platforms to lift the wearer's shoes and give him extra height or alter his gait.

FIBERSCOPE

The FS-100 Fiberscope allowed surveillance of a room by drilling a small hole in a wall and then inserting its flexible tube containing fibre-optic strands into the aperture. These transmitted an image back to a magnifying eyepiece in the grip section, while a lamp built into the device provided illumination.

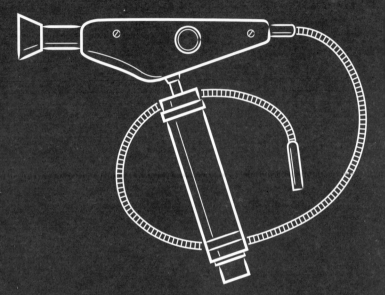

TEAR GAS PEN

This 1948 pen concealed a tear gas round that could be shot up to two metres. The clip rotated slightly to the side to reveal a trigger button, while the barrel unscrewed to allow reloading. An effective defensive weapon, it could debilitate opponents long enough to allow the user to escape.

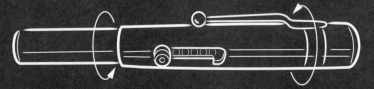